History of the
UNITED STATES I

CLEP* Test Study Guide

All rights reserved. This Study Guide, Book and Flashcards are protected under the US Copyright Law. No part of this book or study guide or flashcards may be reproduced, distributed or stored in a retrieval system, or transmitted in any form or by any means, electronic, mechanical, photocopying, recording, or otherwise, without the prior written permission of the publisher Breely Crush Publishing, LLC.

© 2026 Breely Crush Publishing, LLC

*CLEP is a registered trademark of the College Entrance Examination Board which does not endorse this book.

971010420143

Copyright ©2003 - 2026, Breely Crush Publishing, LLC.

All rights reserved.

This Study Guide, Book and Flashcards are protected under the US Copyright Law. No part of this publication may be reproduced, distributed or stored in a retrieval system, or transmitted in any form or by any means, electronic, mechanical, photocopying, recording, or otherwise, without the prior written permission of the publisher Breely Crush Publishing, LLC.

Published by Breely Crush Publishing, LLC
10808 River Front Parkway
South Jordan, UT 84095
www.breelycrushpublishing.com

ISBN-10: 1-61433-652-0
ISBN-13: 978-1-61433-652-5

Printed and bound in the United States of America.

*CLEP is a registered trademark of the College Entrance Examination Board which does not endorse this book.

Table of Contents

Columbus and Early Explorers 1
Colonization 2
The First English Colony - Jamestown 2
Bacon's Rebellion 3
The Plymouth Company 4
The Puritans - Massachusetts Bay Company 5
The Rhode Island Colony 6
The Connecticut Colony 6
The Maine and New Hampshire Colonies 6
The New York and New Jersey Colonies 6
The Pennsylvania Colony 7
The Maryland Colony 8
The North and South Carolina Colonies 8
The Georgia Colony 8
Life in the Colonies 9
The Salem Witch Trials 9
The Beginning of Slavery 10
The Age of Enlightenment 10
The Great Awakening 11
Manifest Destiny 12
Mercantile System 12
English Acts to Regain Control 12
The French and Indian War 17
1763 to 1789 – The Saga of the Struggle for Independence 17
Samuel Adams 18
The Boston Tea Party 19
The Revolution Begins 20
Common Sense and Independence 21
Franco-American Alliance 23
Victory and Independence 24
The Significance of the American Revolution 25
Creating a Government 26
Fledgling American Democracy (1789-1850) 28
Slavery, Fight for Equality, Civil War and Reunification 30
Black Slavery, Agrarianism and Abolitionism 30
Introduction to the Court Opinion on the Dred Scott Case 31
Dred Scott v. Sandford (1857) 32
The American Civil War 38
*Political Institutions, Political Developments, Behavior and Public
   Policy* 38

The Content of the Constitution *40*
The Ten Original Amendments *41*
How to Make Amendments to the Constitution *44*
Founding Fathers *46*
George Washington's Farewell Address *49*
Monroe Doctrine *57*
The Exponential Growth of the United States, Socially, Economically and
    Culturally *57*
Sample Test Questions *62*
Test-Taking Strategies *95*
What Your Score Means *95*
Test Preparation *96*
Legal Note *96*

 Columbus and Early Explorers

During 1500's the Aztec Empire reigned supreme in the New World with the Mayas, Toltecs and Incas. Each tribe was eventually conquered by the conquerors also known as Conquistadors. The most famous Conquistadores were:

- Hernando Cortez – conquered the Aztecs
- Francisco Pizarro – conquered the Incas

Native Americans had lived in America for thousands of years before the New World was discovered by settlers.

In the year 1492, Christopher Columbus, under patronage from King Ferdinand and Queen Isabella from Spain, left to establish a sea-route to the Far East. The primary goal was to establish a trade route to India, which was prosperous at that time, and also spread Christianity. He sailed with three ships, the *Nina*, the *Pinta* and the *Santa Maria*. Instead of landing in India, he fortuitously landed in the Bahamas where he named the people he found there 'los indios' because he believed he had found an outlying island in the East Indies. He never knew that the land mass he discovered would subsequently come to be known as The New World.

France sent an exploration party under Jacques Cartier who explored along the St. Lawrence River in the year 1534 and the French Government claimed that part of North America. Before the French, in the year 1513, Ponce de Leon, a Spanish Explorer, landed in the area which is today known as Florida. In 1539, the Spanish sent another expedition, which explored along the Mississippi river and landed in Memphis.

In 1565, another expedition under Pedro Menendez de Aviles landed in Florida and started to fortify it. 1606, North America was in total wilderness save for a small group of Spaniards who occupied a small fort at St. Augustine, Florida. Four years later, the Spanish founded Santa Fe in 1610. In 1609 the Dutch founded a site along the Hudson River, which is today known as Albany, N.Y.

This time, before the English began colonizing the New World, became known as the Age of Exploration or the Age of Exploitation or the Age of Conquest. While areas were in fact discovered and explored, conquistadors exploited the Natives they found through slave labor, rape and murder. Wars were fought and civilizations were conquered.

Colonization

Beginning in the fourteen hundreds, Europe began going through a "renaissance", or, rebirth. It was a revival of learning. Roman and Greek scholarship was becoming more valued. Johann Gutenberg invented the movable-type printing press in 1440. With this new invention, it made books and pamphlets available to huge amounts of people. This had been limited in the past for many books were handwritten and therefore very costly.

Colonizing the New World became more important as the populations in Europe increased in huge proportions. Rulers needed to find a place for these masses to live, many of which were unemployed. With colonizing, the potential for riches in the form of spices, gold and silver. Inflation was rising Europe from the increase in gold and silver plundered from the new lands. Because England did not yet have colonies and explorers in the New World, they were at a disadvantage in the economic market.

Sir Walter Raleigh, one of Queen Elizabeth's favorites, was interested in the American land-mass. Having failed in an earlier expedition - 1585 under Grenville and Lane - he sent not just men but entire families to North America in May 1587, and the shipload of people landed in a colony named Roanoke in late July. The wife of Ananias Dare gave birth to a female child and the baby was named Virginia Dare. She was the first English child born in the New World. It was three years later another ship arrived to find the entire colony abandoned. Historians still do not know what happened to this colony. Speculations are that disease, want of supplies and fierce attacks from the Native Indians caused the entire colony was lost.

Colonizing the New World was very expensive, so to share the cost, the English created joint-stock companies. In this investment, individuals shared the risk and the benefits of sending colonists to the New World. The Virginia Company was able to secure patents from the monarchy that gave them monopolies to land.

The First English Colony - Jamestown

In the year 1606 King James of England offered two business companies, The London Company and the Plymouth Company, the right to settle and trade along the Atlantic Coast. The London Company secured the right to settle all the land from what is presently known as Cape Fear, North Carolina, northward to Long Island.

The Plymouth Company got the right to settle all the land from what is today known as Maine southward to Chesapeake Bay.

The London Company sent 120 men in three ships under Captain Christopher Newport, who sailed between two capes of land into the mouth of Chesapeake Bay. In 1607 Newport named the Capes, Cape Henry and Cape Charles, in honor of King James's two sons. He then sailed into a river which he named the James, in honor of the Monarch himself. He sailed further about 30 miles up the river and anchored in a marshy island, which became Jamestown; Virginia, the first established English Colony.

Jamestown settlers faced many obstacles including disease, starvation, and altercations with the Native Americans. Explorer John Smith's leadership and military skill sustained the colony for two years until another English ship arrived. Unfortunately, planning had not been done for these new settlers. Over 400 people arrived without supplies. John Smith became frustrated and returned to England.

Without their leader, Jamestown began its starving time. Over 450 colonists remained, stripping the colony and surroundings of firewood and food. They barricaded themselves in their fort to avoid hostile natives. When regular food supplies were gone, they began to eat anything that was left inside the walls, rats, dogs, livestock, and eventually other humans. In the spring, new settlers and ships with supplies strengthened the colony. The colony continued to struggle until John Rolfe discovered a new commodity, tobacco.

Tobacco could not be grown and sold fast enough. Europe and England were greedy and were huge consumers of it. England decreed that only they would receive the tobacco, and in turn sell it from their ports in England. The monarchy, the investors and the colonists all began to reap the rewards of tobacco. Some colonists returned on the ships with black indentured servants. These servants were not slaves but had pledged to work for an individual for a certain amount of time, usually seven years, in exchange for being brought to the New World. These servants became the first Africans in North America.

 Bacon's Rebellion

Bacon's Rebellion is most importantly known as the first time independent initiative was shown in the colonies. In 1676 colonists in Virginia had been attacked by the Native Americans. Sir William Berkeley, the royal governor, had investigated and arranged meetings between the colonists and the Indians. Nathaniel Bacon was unhappy with this decision. He and others felt that the government should be protecting them. A group was formed and began attacking Indian camps in the area. Known or unknown to the group, different tribes of Indians were peaceful and aggressive. The group mainly attacked peaceful groups. Sir William Berkeley announced that Bacon was a rebel. Bacon's men then forced Berkeley to leave the city. Soon after, Bacon died and Berkeley returned to the colony. Many individuals of the Bacon's group were then hung for punishment. Again, what makes Bacon's Rebellion so important in American History is that it is the first time that the people took matters into their own hands. The idea that you could change your future or your destiny apart from the governing bodies decisions was a new concept to the colonies and this is the first time it was ever shown there.

The Plymouth Company

A group of Separatists, also known as the Pilgrims, wanted to be disentangled from the web of the Church of England and worship God in their own way and sought out the New World for that purpose.

The English Government brought in a law that effectively compelled all citizens to attend the Church of England. The pilgrims refused to obey that dictate and fearing reprisals they fled to Holland in 1608.

The pilgrims were allowed by the Dutch to worship God as they liked, but after a year, the pilgrims decided to move towards America. They were enlisted by a company of English businessmen for settling in America. They were allowed to come only after they agreed to work for at least seven years for the company in the New World.

On September 16, 1620, a ship named the *Mayflower* with one hundred one Pilgrims headed for America. By the 19th of November 1620, they landed in Cape Cod, known today's harbor of Provincetown).

The Pilgrims lived on their ship the *Mayflower* through the winter, while they built homes on their new land. As with most settlers, about half of the colony perished during the winter. These settlers were able to make peace with their Native American neighbors, unlike so many other groups. The Wampanoag Indians helped the Pilgrims survive. Squanto, an Indian, helped the Pilgrims grow maize (corn) the next year.

Pilgrims celebrated their first harvest with the Wampanoag Indians, thanking them for their help in establishing the colony. This is where the tradition of the modern day Thanksgiving originated.

The Pilgrims also formed their own government called the Mayflower Compact. The Pilgrims elected a simple government and pledged to obey their own created laws. This was a first big step towards democracy and self-government.

In 1608 new settlers arrived. The ensuing winter claimed many lives. By the spring of 1610 another batch of settlers arrived. The London Company made each settler responsible for fifty acres or more of land. They gave a small portion of what they grew on the lands to the common storehouse and retained the balance. The London Company, in the year 1619, decided to give the setters a share in their government. There were more than 1000 settlers in Virginia by then. In 1621, the London Company decided to send the first shipload of women to assist the men in the settlements and rear children.

The Puritans - Massachusetts Bay Company

The Pilgrims were followed by the Puritans. They were also not very happy with the Church of England, though they remained members. They wanted to purify and simplify the Church and hence were known as Puritans. They were different from the Pilgrims in that the Pilgrims were more extreme in their beliefs in the Anglican Church. The Puritans believed that the church needed reform, so they were also known as Reformists.

In 1629, the Puritans obtained a charter from the King of England which gave them a grant of land in New England. They also received the right to build a colony. Their company was known as the Massachusetts Bay Company.

In 1628, a shipload of Puritans moved to New England. Some of them started the village of Naumkoag, which later became Salem while others settled in what would become Boston. By the spring of 1630 a large group of Puritans on board a large convoy of ships brought in more than 1,000 men, women and children to the New World.

The Puritans elected John Winthrop to lead the new colony. He led the colony until his death, 20 years later. John Winthrop gave a sermon on a ship while on the way to the New World. This sermon was entitled "City Upon a Hill" also known as "A Model of Christian Charity." This sermon was based on a scripture in the Bible, Matthew 5:14, "You are the light of the world. A city set on a hill cannot be hid." He called to all the colonists to be an example to the rest of the world of how a city should live, becoming a beacon of righteousness to the entire world.

Soon after the Puritans had created their home in the New World, there was a change in how church membership was conferred. In 1622, the "Halfway Covenants" were created to give some people limited church privileges such as baptizing their children. In 1677, this was totally adopted and swelled the sizes of the congregations.

# The Rhode Island Colony

In 1631, Roger Williams reached New England and became friendly with Narragansett's Indians. He also preached in Salem's Church. Puritan leaders created trouble for him and he had to flee to the Indian colony. In 1644 the King of England gave a charter for the colony of Rhode Island to Roger Williams. Rhode Island was seen as a model of freedom.

# The Connecticut Colony

In the year 1636, a dedicated group of people from the Massachusetts Bay colony settled in the banks of the Connecticut River. Thomas Hooker, the Pastor of their Church, led them westward and built a village known as Hartford. The British Monarch, in 1662 AD, gave a charter to the Connecticut colonists, which gave them the right to govern themselves.

# The Maine and New Hampshire Colonies

In 1622, the English King gave Sir Ferdinando Gorges and John Mason the right to settle a vast area which in due course became the states of Maine and New Hampshire. After sometime, George took control of Maine and Mason took control of the New Hampshire area. Settlers from Massachusetts settled many villages and towns in Maine. However, Massachusetts claimed the whole area and Maine never became an independent colony.

# The New York and New Jersey Colonies

In the year 1609, the Dutch East India Company sent Henry Hudson in the ship *Half Moon* along with men to explore the Atlantic coast of the North American continent. His mission was to find a shorter route through America to East India. He failed, but he did find two rivers, the Delaware and Hudson, the river that bears the captain's name.

The Dutch claimed the entire area and named it the New Netherlands. They built a large fort in an island at the mouth of Hudson River and called it New Amsterdam. The Indians who lived there called that area "Mannahatta" (the heavenly land). In 1626 Peter Minute, the governor, bought all the adjoining areas from the Indians for less than twenty-five dollars!

In 1638 Swedish Ships sailed into the Delaware River. They settled in a landmass now known as Wilmington, and named it Fort Christina after their Queen. They settled many adjoining areas and competed with the Dutch. The Dutch resented competition and in 1655 the Dutch army took control of all Swedish Settlements.

We know that the King of England gave a charter to settle lands which were held by the Dutch to the London Company. The English resented the growth of New Netherlands and told the Dutch that the very land they possessed in fact belonged to England. In 1644, English warships roared into the harbor of New Netherlands. The governor of the Dutch, Peter Stuyvesant, on seeing the vast army of the English, brought down the Dutch Flag from the post where it had flown merrily for the preceding fifty years. No shots were fired and the English took over New Netherlands.

The King gave New Netherlands to his brother, James, the Duke of York. The Duke named it New York and the city of New Amsterdam was re-named New York City. The Duke also gave some portion of the lands to his close friends Lord John Berkeley and Sir George Carteret. Once a governor of Jersey in the English Channel, Sir Carteret named the colony New Jersey.

 The Pennsylvania Colony

William Penn was born to a wealthy Admiral of the English Navy. He was endowed with a good heart and a helping hand. He believed everyone had a right to worship. He joined the Society of Friends or Quakers. Quakers believed in the equality of men and they never removed their hats to another person, even when the King was present. At the demise of his father William Penn became a rich man. He wanted to build a separate colony for Quakers in America. King Charles II owed a large sum of money to Penn's father. He said he would allot a piece of land for Penn in America and write off the loan the King owned to Penn's father. In 1681, the King gave Penn a large stretch of land west of Delaware River. The King named the area Penn's Woods or Pennsylvania, which was, of course, in honor of Penn's father. Penn was not happy as the area did not have any abutting coastline. In 1682, the Duke of York gave Penn a grant of land South of Pennsylvania on Delaware Bay. Known previously as lower Counties, it was now called Delaware. The first group of Quakers settled on the banks of the Delaware River and named the colony Philadelphia - the city of Brotherly Love.

 The Maryland Colony

George Calvert, a close friend of King Charles I, wanted to build a colony for all Christians to worship peacefully and in their own way. A large tract of land was given to him north of Virginia. He could not realize his dream as he departed to his heavenly abode. His son, Cecilius, the second Lord Baltimore carried on with his father's wishes. He named the colony Maryland in honor of the wife of King Charles I whose name was Henrietta Maria. The first group of about 200 settlers, both Catholics and Protestants, started settling in the land near the mouth of the Potomac River and named their colony St. Mary's.

 The North and South Carolina Colonies

Settlers from Virginia moved southward into the wild unsettled lands. There was no government and they hunted, caught fish and raised crops. They were hard working. In 1663, the King named this area Carolina. He offered it to eight of his close friends, who were wealthy. They offered land to settlers on easy terms. The southern area of Carolina received a lot of settlers who built a seaport naming it Charles Town, later called Charleston, which became a beehive of activity.

To raise tobacco plantations in Maryland, Virginia as well as the northern part of Carolina proved to be a thriving business, but governing it became arduous. The settlers brought in slaves from Africa. The settlers, then, returned it to the King who bifurcated it into two Royal colonies. In the year 1721, South Carolina, and in 1729, North Carolina were created by the King of England.

 The Georgia Colony

In 1732, James Oglethorpe, a wealthy Englishman, started the last of the English colonies in America along the coast of the Atlantic Ocean. He had a novel idea. Most of the debtors, who could not repay their loans to the creditors, were in prison, and most of them were poor but honest. Oglethorpe wanted to build a colony for such debtors in prison. In 1732 the King of England gave Oglethorpe and some of his own close friends a vast tract of land as a grant. The land was sandwiched between South Carolina and the Spanish colony of Florida. They named it Georgia. In 1733 James Oglethorpe led the first group of debtors selected from English Prisons and settled them in a landmass known as Savannah. Fifty acres of land were given to each settler. No alcoholic beverages and no slavery were allowed in Georgia - a model colony indeed! Savannah became a thriving seaport. In the year 1752, Georgia was declared a Royal colony.

In 1606 there were no settlers in the American continent, save the natives. In less than 150 years, England ruled in 13 colonies along the east coast. Nearly 2 million people lived in the 13 colonies. They, in fact, were in the process of constructing a viable New Nation, a Nation that was destined to be the most powerful country in the world in time to come!

Life in the Colonies

Life in the Northern colonies differed greatly from the Southern colonies. In fact, each colony was very different, centered around many different values and beliefs. The Northern colonies were formed around the church, literally. Each church was surrounded by houses and a "green" or "commons" where trade and other activities took place. The houses and colony life revolved around the church. Church and state were one in the Northern colonies.

In the Southern colonies, people were spread out on large plantations, far away from each other. The Southern colonies made their money from the plantations which took a lot of manpower to work. They had many indentured servants perform labor and eventually began purchasing slaves to help with the labor. Although many considered themselves religious, few went to church regularly and some people never attended. The colonists living in the Southern colonies imitated the rich in England and created their own social structures.

The Salem Witch Trials

The Salem Witch Trials began when a group of teenage girls accused middle aged women in the Salem community of witchcraft. Because people were still superstitious at the time, this epidemic spread like wildfire. Over 300 women were convicted of witchcraft and more than nineteen of them were hanged with no proof.

Historians have since determined that the accusations arisen between two different social groups. Women who lived outside the norm of a woman's perceived role at the time, who were unmarried or worked outside the home, were targeted.

The Beginning of Slavery

The Portuguese were the first to import black slaves into the New World. They began with sugar plantations and then moved many more into mining for gold and silver.

Spain, England, Holland and France all participated in the buying and selling of slaves.

The Triangular Trade was known as shipping lines that connected Europe, Africa and the America's with slaves. Slaves were also forced to endure a "seasoning" process where they were prepared for sale. About 30% of slaves died during this seasoning process.

Location	Exports
Africa	Slaves
West Indies	Sugar, Molasses & Rum
England	Manufactured Goods
American Colonies	Fish, Grain, Flour & Lumber

All colonies had legalized slavery by 1750. Rising wages for indentured servants made slaves popular. Colonies developed laws to keep slaves under control. They restricted slaves of:

- Right to assembly
- Earning money
- Seek after an education
- Autonomy of movement

Many unspeakable acts were legal to perform on slaves under certain circumstances. The white colonists feared a slave revolt. Their livelihood depended on the willing or unwilling work of their slaves. Two slave revolts, one in South Carolina and one in New York, made slave owners more anxious than ever before.

The Age of Enlightenment

The Age of Enlightenment was a scientific revolution. Scientists now believed that the sun was the center of the universe. Isaac Newton published his theory of gravity. More and more people were using critical reasoning and scientific thought to question the way things were and the way things were done.

This was the beginning seeds of the American Dream: that all people can excel and succeed if they work hard. This was a far cry from the caste system that someone was born into. In the caste system, if you were born to a fisherman, you would be a fisherman or other tradesman and marry the children of the same. Very rarely did people cross classes, marrying up or down. Status could not be changed easily.

John Locke created an idea called Theory of Contract under Natural Law. The idea was the kings, queens, princes, etc., were not divinely determined by God but instead were just born lucky. He believed that all people had natural rights to life, liberty and happiness. Locke had a great influence on the people, in fact, much of his ideas appeared in the Declaration of Independence when Thomas Jefferson wrote that everyone had a right to "life, liberty and the pursuit of happiness."

The Great Awakening

The Great Awakening, 1730s, was a time when religion, which had been put on the back burner, became very prominent and important again. Many important preachers contributed to this new excitement for religion.

George Whitefield was a young twenty-seven year old man who preached to thousands of people at a time. He believed that the people lacked passion because "dead men preach to them." Whitefield created dramas and skits about the pleasures of heaven and the pains of hell. He used entertainment to draw and keep his congregations.

Jonathan Edwards did not use entertainment to draw his congregation. He talked of fire and brimstone, trying to scare his flock into choosing what was right. One of his sermons "Sinners in the Hands of an Angry God" is one of the most famous sermons in American history.

The Great Awakening did more than get the colonists into church. It also stimulated an interest in reading and spurred the distribution of books and the creation of schools and libraries. The Great Awakening was the beginning of the separation of church and state.

 Manifest Destiny

Colonists believed that America was destined to grow and colonize west. This was thought of as a divine right and stewardship.

 Mercantile System

Spain, England, France, Portugal and other European countries believed in a mercantile system. Power was linked to wealth and wealth was linked to trade. Each country encouraged their manufacturing plants to create as many goods as possible and tried to protect their own industries. England forbade the colonies to ship their good anywhere but England, so a tax could be added before exported.

 English Acts to Regain Control

Until the 1750s, the colonies had been virtually ignored by England. This was called the Age of Salutary Neglect. New tariffs or taxes were not imposed and those that existed were not enforced.

The Navigation Act of 1660 determined that goods from the colonies could only be transported by English Ships. It also restricted colonies from exporting or trading certain goods within the colonies or England.

The Restraining Acts of 1699 restricted the colonies from building factories. It also restricted the export of beaver hats and iron.

The Molasses Act created a huge tax on sugar and molasses imported into the colonies. This act was never strictly enforced. Because the acts were not enforced, it opened the door for colonists to question England.

John Dickenson's *Letters from a Farmer in Pennsylvania* was published and called the colonists to action and awareness of England's policies and taxes.

Common Sense was written by Thomas Paine to show King George III as a tyrannical leader. He wanted colonists to unite to form a truly free company. His words were so compelling that in a little more than a few months of the printing, over 100,000 copies sold.

The following is *Common Sense*. The word usage and or misspellings are original.

"SOME writers have so confounded society with government, as to leave little or no distinction between them; whereas they are not only different, but have different origins. Society is produced by our wants, and government by wickedness; the former promotes our happiness positively by uniting our affections, the latter negatively by restraining our vices. The one encourages intercourse, the other creates distinctions. The first is a patron, the last a punisher.

"Society in every state is a blessing, but government even in its best state is but a necessary evil; in its worst state an intolerable one; for when we suffer, or are exposed to the same miseries by a government, which we might expect in a country without government, our calamity is heightened by reflecting that we furnish the means by which we suffer. Government, like dress, is the badge of lost innocence; the palaces of kings are built on the ruins of the bowers of paradise. For were the impulses of conscience clear, uniform, and irresistibly obeyed, man would need no other lawgiver; but that not being the case, he finds it necessary to surrender up a part of his property to furnish means for the protection of the rest; and this he is induced to do by the same prudence which in every other case advises him out of two evils to choose the least. Wherefore, security being the true design and end of government, it unanswerably follows that whatever form thereof appears most likely to ensure it to us, with the least expense and greatest benefit, is preferable to all others.

"In order to gain a clear and just idea of the design and end of government, let us suppose a small number of persons settled in some sequestered part of the earth, unconnected with the rest, they will then represent the first peopling of any country, or of the world. In this state of natural liberty, society will be their first thought. A thousand motives will excite them thereto, the strength of one man is so unequal to his wants, and his mind so unfitted for perpetual solitude, that he is soon obliged to seek assistance and relief of another, who in his turn requires the same. Four or five united would be able to raise a tolerable dwelling in the midst of a wilderness, but one man might labour out the common period of life without accomplishing anything; when he had felled his timber he could not remove it, nor erect it after it was removed; hunger in the meantime would urge him from his work, and every different want call him a different way. Disease, nay even misfortune would be death, for though neither might be mortal, yet either would disable him from living, and reduce him to a state in which he might rather be said to perish than to die.

"This necessity, like a gravitating power, would soon form our newly arrived emigrants into society, the reciprocal blessing of which, would supersede, and render the obligations of law and government unnecessary while they remained perfectly just to each other; but as nothing but heaven is impregnable to vice, it will unavoidably happen, that in proportion as they surmount the first difficulties of emigration, which bound them together in a common cause, they will begin to relax in their duty and attachment to each other; and this remissness, will point out the necessity, of establishing some form of government to supply the defect of moral virtue.

"Some convenient tree will afford them a State-House, under the branches of which, the whole colony may assemble to deliberate on public matters. It is more than probable that their first laws will have the title only of REGULATIONS, and be enforced by no other penalty than public disesteem. In this first parliament every man, by natural right, will have a seat.

"But as the colony increases, the public concerns will increase likewise, and the distance at which the members may be separated, will render it too inconvenient for all of them to meet on every occasion as at first, when their number was small, their habitations near, and the public concerns few and trifling. This will point out the convenience of their consenting to leave the legislative part to be managed by a select number chosen from the whole body, who are supposed to have the same concerns at stake which those have who appointed them, and who will act in the same manner as the whole body would act were they present. If the colony continues increasing, it will become necessary to augment the number of the representatives, and that the interest of every part of the colony may be attended to, it will be found best to divide the whole into convenient parts, each part sending its proper number; and that the elected might never form to themselves an interest separate from the electors, prudence will point out the propriety of having elections often; because as the elected might by that means return and mix again with the general body of the electors in a few months, their fidelity to the public will be secured by the prudent reflexion of not making a rod for themselves. And as this frequent interchange will establish a common interest with every part of the community, they will mutually and naturally support each other, and on this (not on the unmeaning name of king) depends the strength of government, and the happiness of the governed.

"Here then is the origin and rise of government; namely, a mode rendered necessary by the inability of moral virtue to govern the world; here too is the design and end of government, viz. freedom and security. And however our eyes may be dazzled with snow, or our ears deceived by sound; however prejudice may warp our wills, or interest darken our understanding, the simple voice of nature and of reason will say, it is right.

"I draw my idea of the form of government from a principle in nature, which no art can overturn, viz. that the more simple any thing is, the less liable it is to be disordered, and the easier repaired when disordered; and with this maxim in view, I offer a few remarks on the so much boasted constitution of England. That it was noble for the dark and slavish times in which it was erected, is granted. When the world was over run with tyranny the least remove therefrom was a glorious rescue. But that it is imperfect, subject to convulsions, and incapable of producing what it seems to promise, is easily demonstrated.

"Absolute governments (tho' the disgrace of human nature) have this advantage with them, that they are simple; if the people suffer, they know the head from which their suffering springs, know likewise the remedy, and are not bewildered by a variety of causes and cures. But the constitution of England is so exceedingly complex, that the nation may suffer for years together without being able to discover in which part the fault lies, some will say in one and some in another, and every political physician will advise a different medicine.

"I know it is difficult to get over local or long standing prejudices, yet if we will suffer ourselves to examine the component parts of the English constitution, we shall find them to be the base remains of two ancient tyrannies, compounded with some new republican materials.

"First.—The remains of monarchical tyranny in the person of the king.
Secondly.—The remains of aristocratical tyranny in the persons of the peers.
Thirdly.—The new republican materials, in the persons of the commons, on whose virtue depends the freedom of England.
"The two first, by being hereditary, are independent of the people; wherefore in a constitutional sense they contribute nothing towards the freedom of the state.
To say that the constitution of England is a union of three powers reciprocally checking each other, is farcical, either the words have no meaning, or they are flat contradictions.
To say that the commons is a check upon the king, presupposes two things.
First.—That the king is not to be trusted without being looked after, or in other words, that a thirst for absolute power is the natural disease of monarchy.
Secondly.—That the commons, by being appointed for that purpose, are either wiser or more worthy of confidence than the crown.

"But as the same constitution which gives the commons a power to check the king by withholding the supplies, gives afterwards the king a power to check the commons, by empowering him to reject their other bills; it again supposes that the king is wiser than those whom it has already supposed to be wiser than him. A mere absurdity!

"There is something exceedingly ridiculous in the composition of monarchy; it first excludes a man from the means of information, yet empowers him to act in cases where the highest judgment is required. The state of a king shuts him from the world, yet the business of a king requires him to know it thoroughly; wherefore the different parts, by unnaturally opposing and destroying each other, prove the whole character to be absurd and useless.

"Some writers have explained the English constitution thus; the king, say they, is one, the people another; the peers are an house in behalf of the king; the commons in behalf of the people; but this hath all the distinctions of an house divided against itself; and though the expressions be pleasantly arranged, yet when examined they appear idle and ambiguous; and it will always happen, that the nicest construction that words are capable of, when applied to the description of some thing which either cannot exist, or is too incomprehensible to be within the compass of description, will be words of sound only, and though they may amuse the ear, they cannot inform the mind, for this explanation includes a previous question, viz. How came the king by a power which the people are afraid to trust, and always obliged to check? Such a power could not be the gift of a wise people, neither can any power, which needs checking, be from God; yet the provision, which the constitution makes, supposes such a power to exist.

"But the provision is unequal to the task; the means either cannot or will not accomplish the end, and the whole affair is a felo de se; for as the greater weight will always carry up the less, and as all the wheels of a machine are put in motion by one, it only remains to know which power in the constitution has the most weight, for that will govern; and though the others, or a part of them, may clog, or, as the phrase is, check the rapidity of its motion, yet so long as they cannot stop it, their endeavors will be ineffectual; the first moving power will at last have its way, and what it wants in speed is supplied by time.

"That the crown is this overbearing part in the English constitution needs not be mentioned, and that it derives its whole consequence merely from being the giver of places and pensions is self-evident; wherefore, though we have been wise enough to shut and lock a door against absolute monarchy, we at the same time have been foolish enough to put the crown in possession of the key.

"The prejudice of Englishmen, in favour of their own government by king, lords and commons, arises as much or more from national pride than reason. Individuals are undoubtedly safer in England than in some other countries, but the will of the king is as much the law of the land in Britain as in France, with this difference, that instead of proceeding directly from his mouth, it is handed to the people under the more formidable shape of an act of parliament. For the fate of Charles the first, hath only made kings more subtle—not more just.

"Wherefore, laying aside all national pride and prejudice in favour of modes and forms, the plain truth is, that it is wholly owing to the constitution of the people, and not to the constitution of the government that the crown is not as oppressive in England as in Turkey.

"An inquiry into the constitutional errors in the English form of government is at this time highly necessary; for as we are never in a proper condition of doing justice to others, while we continue under the influence of some leading partiality, so neither are we capable of doing it to ourselves while we remain fettered by any obstinate prejudice. And as a man, who is attached to a prostitute, is unfitted to choose or judge of a wife, so any prepossession in favour of a rotten constitution of government will disable us from discerning a good one."

 ## The French and Indian War

The English colonies were often fought with the French, who were settled in the St. Lawrence Valley, the Mississippi Valley, as well as the Great Lake area, over fishing and trade.

The French and Indian Natives on the one side and the English settlers on the other side started a war in the year 1754. It spread to Europe in 1756. The French could not withstand the might of the English and lost the war.

The "Treaty of Paris" was signed in 1763 and brought the war to a halt in the New World. As a result Canada and all other French colonies east of Mississippi came under English Rule.

Spain gave Florida to the English in exchange for all the land west of the Mississippi.

The supremacy of the English in the New World was firmly established. The English language prevailed.

 ## 1763 to 1789 – The Saga of the Struggle for Independence

Because of the battles with the French for extended periods, the American colonies and England grew close, and there prevailed a healthy and friendly relationship.

For over 150 years the colonies developed their own society, value systems, economy, and attempts at self-governance. England did not interfere in the settlements' affairs. They first provided security by keeping the British Armies in the settlements. But after 1763 and the Treaty of Paris, there was a perceptible change in the British policy towards the colonies. Direct taxes were levied. More and more coercive restrictions on manufacturing and trade were slapped on. Colonial assemblies and local governments enjoyed, hitherto, the right to tax. They did not like England interfering with their rights. They appealed for their rights; not for independence. The answer from King George III of Great Britain was a cascade of more stringent restrictions. More troops were sent to maintain law and order and enforce the new measures strictly.

These measures forced the colonies to think in terms of gaining total independence from England. In 1765, a Quartering Act demanded colonies to provide housing and supplies to British troops. This was followed by another act, the Stamp Act. On the basis of this Act a direct tax on business instruments, licenses, legal documents and on newspapers was levied. Due to extreme resentment shown by the colonies, this stamp act was repealed in the year 1766. However, new taxes, Townsend Duties on glass, lead - paint, paper and imported tea, were levied. Colonies resented these British coercive measures.

They wanted to preserve their thirst for right, liberty, duty and dignity, which over the years had become the hallmark of the American people. In 1770, the Townsend duties were revoked. Only a tax on tea remained. From 1771 to 1773 there was increasing tension between the colonies and Britain.

Samuel Adams

During a three-year interval of calm, a relatively small number of radicals strove energetically to keep the controversy alive. They contended that payment of the tax constituted an acceptance of the principle that Parliament had the right to rule over the colonies. They feared that at any time in the future, the principle of Parliamentary rule might be applied with devastating effect on all colonial liberties.

The radicals' most effective leader was Samuel Adams of Massachusetts, who toiled tirelessly for a single end: independence from England. From the time he graduated from Harvard College in 1743, Adams was a public servant in some capacity - inspector of chimneys, tax collector, and moderator of town meetings. A consistent failure in business, he was shrewd and able in politics, with the New England town meeting his theater of action.

Adams wanted to free people from their awe of social and political superiors, make them aware of their own power and importance, and thus arouse them to action. To reach these objectives, he published articles in newspapers and made speeches in town meetings, instigating resolutions that appealed to the colonists' democratic impulses.

In 1772 he induced the Boston town meeting to select a "Committee of Correspondence" to state the rights and grievances of the colonists. The committee opposed a British decision to pay the salaries of judges from customs revenues; it feared that the judges would no longer be dependent on the legislature for their incomes and thus no longer accountable to it, thereby leading to the emergence of "a despotic form of government." The committee communicated with other towns on this matter and requested them to draft replies. Committees were set up in virtually all the colonies, and out of them grew a base of effective revolutionary organizations. Still, Adams did not have enough fuel to set a fire.

 The Boston Tea Party

In 1773, however, Britain furnished Adams and his allies with an incendiary issue. The powerful East India Company, finding itself in critical financial straits, appealed to the British government, which granted it a monopoly on all tea exported to the colonies. The government also permitted the East India Company to supply retailers directly, bypassing colonial wholesalers. By then, most of the tea consumed in America was imported illegally, duty-free. By selling its tea through its own agents at a price well under the customary one, the East India Company made smuggling unprofitable and threatened to eliminate the independent colonial merchants. Aroused not only by the loss of the tea trade but also by the monopolistic practice involved, colonial traders joined the radicals agitating for independence.

In ports up and down the Atlantic coast, agents of the East India Company were forced to resign. New shipments of tea were either returned to England or warehoused. In Boston, however, the agents defied the colonists; with the support of the royal governor, they made preparations to land incoming cargoes regardless of opposition. On the night of December 16, 1773, a band of men disguised as Mohawk Indians and led by Samuel Adams boarded three British ships lying at anchor and dumped their tea cargo into Boston harbor. Doubting their countrymen's commitment to principle, they feared that if the tea were landed, colonists would actually purchase the tea and pay the tax.

A crisis now confronted Britain. The East India Company had carried out a parliamentary statute. If the destruction of the tea went unpunished, Parliament would admit to the world that it had no control over the colonies. Official opinion in Britain almost unanimously condemned the Boston Tea Party as an act of vandalism and advocated legal measures to bring the insurgent colonists into line.

In 1773 a new tea act was passed by England in their Parliament. This lead to the first ever open resistance to English Rule, 342 tea chests were thrown into the sea from the anchored British ships in Boston. This resulted in the British passing the Five Intolerable Acts, in the year 1774. The first continental congress of the colonies met at Philadelphia and declared the Five Intolerable Acts as unconstitutional. The first battle took place in Massachusetts in the year 1775. The America Revolution, the war to end an oppressive regime, and with it, to end colonialism, had begun.

The Revolution Begins

General Thomas Gage, an amiable English gentleman with an American-born wife, commanded the garrison at Boston, where political activity had almost wholly replaced trade. Gage's main duty in the colonies had been to enforce the Coercive Acts. When news reached him that the Massachusetts colonists were collecting powder and military stores at the town of Concord, thirty-two kilometers away, Gage sent a strong detail to confiscate these munitions.

After a night of marching, the British troops reached the village of Lexington on April 19, 1775, and saw a grim band of seventy-seven Minutemen - so named because they were said to be ready to fight in a minute - through the early morning mist. The Minutemen intended only a silent protest, but Marine Major John Pitcairn, the leader of the British troops, yelled, "Disperse, you damned rebels! You dogs, run!" The leader of the Minutemen, Captain John Parker, told his troops not to fire unless fired at first. The Americans were withdrawing when someone fired a shot, which led the British troops to fire at the Minutemen. The British then charged with bayonets, leaving eight dead and ten wounded. In the often-quoted phrase of 19th century poet Ralph Waldo Emerson, this was "the shot heard round the world."

The British pushed on to Concord. The Americans had taken away most of the munitions, but they destroyed whatever was left. In the meantime, American forces in the countryside had mobilized to harass the British on their long return to Boston. All along the road, behind stone walls, hillocks, and houses, militiamen from "every Middlesex village and farm" made targets of the bright red coats of the British soldiers. By the time Gage's weary detachment stumbled into Boston, it had suffered more than 250 killed and wounded. The Americans lost ninety-three men.

The Second Continental Congress met in Philadelphia, Pennsylvania, on May 10th. The Congress voted to go to war, inducting the colonial militias into continental service. It appointed Colonel George Washington of Virginia as their commander-in-chief on June 15th. Within two days, the Americans had incurred high casualties at Bunker Hill just outside Boston. Congress also ordered American expeditions to march northward into Canada by fall. Capturing Montreal, they failed in a winter assault on Quebec, and eventually retreated to New York.

Despite the outbreak of armed conflict, the idea of complete separation from England was still repugnant to many members of the Continental Congress. In July, it adopted the Olive Branch Petition, begging the King to prevent further hostile actions until some sort of agreement could be worked out. King George rejected it; instead, on August 23, 1775, he issued a proclamation declaring the colonies to be in a state of rebellion.

Britain had expected the Southern colonies to remain loyal, in part because of their reliance on slavery. Many in the Southern colonies feared that a rebellion against the mother country would also trigger a slave uprising. In November 1775, Lord Dunmore, the governor of Virginia, tried to capitalize on that fear by offering freedom to all slaves who would fight for the British. Instead, his proclamation drove to the rebel side many Virginians who would otherwise have remained Loyalist.

The governor of North Carolina, Josiah Martin, also urged North Carolinians to remain loyal to the Crown. When 1,500 men answered Martin's call, they were defeated by revolutionary armies before British troops could arrive to help.

British warships continued down the coast to Charleston, South Carolina, and opened fire on the city in early June 1776. But South Carolinians had time to prepare, and repulsed the British by the end of the month. They would not return south for more than two years.

Common Sense and Independence

In January 1776, Thomas Paine, a radical political theorist and writer who had come to America from England in 1774, published a fifty-page pamphlet, *Common Sense*. Within three months, it sold 100,000 copies. Paine attacked the idea of a hereditary monarchy, declaring that one honest man was worth more to society than "all the crowned ruffians that ever lived." He presented the alternatives - continued submission to a tyrannical king and an outworn government, or liberty and happiness as a self-sufficient, independent republic. Circulated throughout the colonies, *Common Sense* helped to crystallize a decision for separation.

There still remained the task, however, of gaining each colony's approval of a formal declaration. On June 7th, Richard Henry Lee of Virginia introduced a resolution in the Second Continental Congress, declaring, "That these United Colonies are, and of right ought to be, free and independent states..." Immediately, a committee of five, headed by Thomas Jefferson of Virginia, was appointed to draft a document for a vote.

Largely Jefferson's work, the Declaration of Independence, adopted July 4, 1776, not only announced the birth of a new nation, but also set forth a philosophy of human freedom that would become a dynamic force throughout the entire world. The Declaration drew upon French and English Enlightenment political philosophy, but one influence in particular stands out: John Locke's Second Treatise on Government. Locke took conceptions of the traditional rights of Englishmen and universalized them into the natural rights of all humankind. The Declaration's familiar opening passage echoes Locke's social contract theory of government:

"We hold these truths to be self-evident, that all men are created equal, that they are endowed by their Creator with certain unalienable Rights, that among these are Life, Liberty and the pursuit of Happiness. -- That to secure these rights, Governments are instituted among Men, deriving their just powers from the consent of the governed, - That whenever any Form of Government becomes destructive of these ends, it is the Right of the People to alter or to abolish it, and to institute new Government, laying its foundation on such principles and organizing its powers in such form, as to them shall seem most likely to affect their Safety and Happiness."

Jefferson linked Locke's principles directly to the situation in the colonies. To fight for American independence was to fight for a government based on popular consent in place of a government by a king who had "combined with others to subject us to a jurisdiction foreign to our constitution, and unacknowledged by our laws..." Only a government based on popular consent could secure natural rights to life, liberty, and the pursuit of happiness. Thus, to fight for American independence was to fight on behalf of one's own natural rights.

DEFEATS AND VICTORIES

Although the Americans suffered severe setbacks for months after independence was declared, their tenacity and perseverance eventually paid off. During August 1776, in the Battle of Long Island in New York, Washington's position became untenable, and he executed a masterly retreat in small boats from Brooklyn to the Manhattan shore. British General William Howe hesitated twice and allowed the Americans to escape. By November, however, Howe had captured Fort Washington on Manhattan Island. New York City would remain under British control until the end of the war.

That December, Washington's forces were near collapse, as supplies and promised aid failed to materialize. Howe again missed his chance to crush the Americans by deciding to wait until spring to resume fighting. On Christmas Day, December 25, 1776, Washington crossed the Delaware River, north of Trenton, New Jersey. In the early-morning hours of December 26th, his troops surprised the British garrison there, taking more than 900 prisoners. A week later, on January 3, 1777, Washington attacked the British at Princeton, regaining most of the territory formally occupied by the British. The victories at Trenton and Princeton revived flagging American spirits.

In September 1777, however, Howe defeated the American army at Brandywine in Pennsylvania and occupied Philadelphia, forcing the Continental Congress to flee. Washington had to endure the bitterly cold winter of 1777 into 1778 at Valley Forge, Pennsylvania, lacking adequate food, clothing, and supplies. Farmers and merchants exchanged their goods for British gold and silver rather than for dubious paper money issued by the Continental Congress and the states.

Valley Forge was the lowest ebb for Washington's Continental Army, but elsewhere the year 1777 proved to be the turning point in the war. British General John Burgoyne, moving south from Canada, attempted to invade New York and New England via Lake Champlain and the Hudson River. He had too much heavy equipment to negotiate the wooded and marshy terrain. On August 6th, at Oriskany, New York, a band of Loyalists and Native Americans under Burgoyne's command ran into a mobile and seasoned American force that managed to halt their advance. A few days later at Bennington, Vermont, more of Burgoyne's forces, seeking much-needed supplies, were pushed back by American troops.

Moving to the west side of the Hudson River, Burgoyne's army advanced on Albany. The Americans were waiting for him. Led by Benedict Arnold - who would later betray the Americans at West Point, New York - the colonials twice repulsed the British. Having by this time incurred heavy losses, Burgoyne fell back to Saratoga, New York, where a vastly superior American force under General Horatio Gates surrounded the British troops. On October 17, 1777, Burgoyne surrendered his entire army - six generals, 300 other officers, and 5,500 enlisted personnel.

Franco-American Alliance

In France, enthusiasm for the American cause was high as the French intellectual world was itself stirring against feudalism and privilege. However, the French crown lent its support to the colonies for geopolitical rather than ideological reasons. The French government had been eager for reprisal against Britain ever since France's defeat in 1763. To further the American cause, Benjamin Franklin was sent to Paris in 1776. His wit, guile, and intellect soon made their presence felt in the French capital, and played a major role in winning French assistance.

France began providing aid to the colonies in May 1776, when it sent fourteen ships with war supplies to America. In fact, most of the gunpowder used by the American armies came from France. After Britain's defeat at Saratoga, France saw an opportunity to seriously weaken its ancient enemy and restore the balance of power that had been upset by the Seven Years' War (called the French and Indian War in the American Colonies). On February 6, 1778, the colonies and France signed a Treaty of Amity and Commerce, in which France recognized the United States as a country and offered trade concessions. They also signed a Treaty of Alliance, which stipulated that if France entered the war, neither country would lay down its arms until the colonies won their independence, and that neither would conclude peace with Britain without the consent of the other, and that each guaranteed the other's possessions in America. This was the only bilateral defense treaty signed by the United States or its predecessors until 1949.

The Franco-American alliance soon broadened the conflict. In June 1778 British ships fired on French vessels, and the two countries went to war. In 1779, Spain, hoping to reacquire territories taken by Britain in the Seven Years' War, entered the conflict on the side of France, but not as an ally of the Americans. In 1780 Britain declared war on the Dutch, who had continued to trade with the Americans. The combination of these European powers, with France in the lead, was a far greater threat to Britain than the American colonies standing alone.

THE BRITISH MOVE SOUTH

With the French now involved, the British, still believing that most Southerners were Loyalists, stepped up their efforts in the Southern colonies. A campaign began in late 1778, with the capture of Savannah, Georgia. Shortly thereafter, British troops and naval forces converged on Charleston, South Carolina, the principal Southern port. They managed to bottle up American forces on the Charleston peninsula. On May 12, 1780, General Benjamin Lincoln surrendered the city and its 5,000 troops, in the greatest American defeat of the war.

But the reversal in fortune only emboldened the American rebels. South Carolinians began roaming the countryside, attacking British supply lines. In July, American General Horatio Gates, who had assembled a replacement force of untrained militiamen, rushed to Camden, South Carolina, to confront British forces led by General Charles Cornwallis. But Gates's makeshift army panicked and ran when confronted by the British regulars. Cornwallis's troops met the Americans several more times, but the most significant battle took place at Cowpens, South Carolina, in early 1781, where the Americans soundly defeated the British. After an exhausting but unproductive chase through North Carolina, Cornwallis set his sights on Virginia.

 Victory and Independence

In July 1780 France's King Louis XVI had sent to America an expeditionary force of 6,000 men under the Comte Jean de Rochambeau. In addition, the French fleet harassed British shipping and blocked reinforcement and resupply of British forces in Virginia. French and American armies and navies, totaling 18,000 men, parried with Cornwallis all through the summer and into the fall. Finally, on October 19, 1781, after being trapped at Yorktown near the mouth of Chesapeake Bay, Cornwallis surrendered his army of 8,000 British soldiers.

Although Cornwallis's defeat did not immediately end the war - which would drag on inconclusively for almost two more years - a new British government decided to pursue peace negotiations in Paris in early 1782, with the American side represented by

Benjamin Franklin, John Adams, and John Jay. On April 15, 1783, Congress approved the final treaty. Signed on September 3rd, the Treaty of Paris acknowledged the independence, freedom, and sovereignty of the thirteen former colonies, now states. The new United States stretched west to the Mississippi River, north to Canada, and south to Florida, which was returned to Spain. The fledgling colonies that Richard Henry Lee had spoken of more than seven years before had finally become "free and independent states." The task of knitting together a nation remained.

The Significance of the American Revolution

The American Revolution had significance far beyond the North American continent. It attracted the attention of a political intelligentsia throughout the European continent. Idealistic nobles such as Thaddeus Kosciusko, Friedrich von Steuben, and the Marquis de Lafayette joined its ranks to affirm liberal ideas they hoped to transfer to their own nations. Its success strengthened the concept of natural rights throughout the Western world and furthered the Enlightenment rationalist critique of an old order built around hereditary monarchy and an established church. In a very real sense, it was a precursor to the French Revolution, but it lacked the French Revolution's violence and chaos because it had occurred in a society that was already fundamentally liberal.

The ideas of the Revolution have been most often depicted as a triumph of the social contract/natural rights theories of John Locke. While this is correct to a certain extent, this characterization passes too quickly over the continuing importance of Calvinist dissenting Protestantism, which from the Pilgrims and Puritans on had also stood for the ideals of the social contract and the self-governing community. Lockean intellectuals and the Protestant clergy were both important advocates of compatible strains of liberalism that had flourished in the British North American colonies.

Scholars have also argued that another persuasion contributed to the Revolution: "republicanism." Republicanism, they assert, did not deny the existence of natural rights but subordinated them to the belief that the maintenance of a free republic required a strong sense of communal responsibility and the cultivation of self-denying virtue among its leaders. The assertion of individual rights, even the pursuit of individual happiness, seemed egoistic by contrast. For a time republicanism threatened to displace natural rights as the major theme of the Revolution. Most historians today, however, concede that the distinction was much overdrawn. Most individuals who thought about such things in the 18th century envisioned the two ideas more as different sides of the same intellectual coin.

Revolution usually entails social upheaval and violence on a wide scale. By this criteria, the American Revolution was relatively mild. About 100,000 Loyalists left the new United States. Some thousands were members of old elites who had suffered expropriation of their property and been expelled; others were simply common people faithful to their King. The majority of those who went into exile did so voluntarily. The Revolution did open up and further liberalize an already liberal society. In New York and the Carolinas, large Loyalist estates were divided among small farmers. Liberal assumptions became the official norm of American political culture - whether in the disestablishment of the Anglican Church, the principle of elected national and state executives, or the wide dissemination of the idea of individual freedom. Yet the structure of society changed little. Revolution or not, most people remained secure in their life, liberty, and property.

Creating a Government

While the form of government adopted by the United States drew heavily on European sources, it was nonetheless distinctly American. The colonists, of course, brought English ideas with them when they crossed the Atlantic, but once here these ideas were slowly but definitely modified to reflect conditions in the New World.

The settlers, like their kin who stayed in England, believed that British government and the common law constituted the greatest protections of individual liberties that had ever existed. The Magna Carta in 1215 had laid down the great root principle of constitutional democracy, the idea that a fundamental law exists beyond which no one, not even the king, may trespass. The rule of law, as it had developed in the centuries between Magna Carta and the first English settlement at Jamestown, came to encompass a parliament and a court system - the first to represent the interests of the people to their rulers, and the second to provide impartial administration of justice. Although the executive power and the symbols of majesty remained with the monarch, the parliament gradually won an important share of power through its control of taxes and the purse. The judicial system achieved its authority by mastery of the intricacies of the law.

The British system, both in theory and in practice, relied on the existence of an upper class, an aristocracy which had the wealth, leisure and education to devote to the problems of governing. In their studies of government, English writers posited a society of distinct classes and interests, all of which would be balanced so that no one part could dominate the others. It was in Parliament that the various groups in society would be represented, look after their own interests, advance the greater interest of the realm and, above all, jealously guard the rights and properties of the people.

It is not surprising that the colonists tried to emulate these institutions when they created their own governments. Moreover, they took with them a few powerful ideas that were then beginning to circulate in the Mother Country, such as the notion which the Puritans had developed of a governing compact or covenant. In the New England colonies especially, the covenant theory became an essential part of political as well as religious thought, expressing the idea that people covenanted with one another to form a government that they were bound to obey, provided it did not exceed the authority granted to it.

In the 169 years between the landing at Jamestown and the signing of the Declaration of Independence, the colonial experience diverged significantly from its English roots. Here there was no established aristocracy; no leisure class could devote itself to government. The settlers looked to those of their neighbors who had talents and abilities for leadership, with the result that the Americans came to see government less as the preserve of the upper classes than as an instrument for all the people. Because colonial society was so fluid, the notion of a parliament representing fixed interests made little sense; moreover, the towns and rural areas that sent representatives to their colonial legislatures gave them directions on how to vote on particular issues. While it is true that a majority of the settlers were disenfranchised because of gender, race or lack of property, the fact remains that popular participation in the political process was far greater in the colonies in the eighteenth century than in the Mother Country.

The Americans, even as they separated from the Crown, nonetheless claimed that all they wanted was their rights as Englishmen. After independence, as they set about creating union and government, they relied on two sources of thought - classic English political theory, and their own experiences. In the Articles of Confederation, the United States' first constitution, the framers relied more on theory, and aimed at creating a federal government that would avoid the problems associated with a strong central government, the very problem that had led to their revolt from Great Britain. But that system proved too weak for the task of governing the new nation, since it lacked sufficient powers. At the Philadelphia convention of 1787, John Dickinson, the chief author of the Articles, urged his fellow delegates: "Experience must be our only guide; reason may mislead us." The Constitution they drafted drew from both reason and experience, and as a result has proven a remarkably durable document.

However the Constitution, even after its adoption in 1788 and the addition of the first ten amendments, the Bill of Rights, in 1791, was little more than an outline of government. The Philadelphia Convention had spelled out certain powers and limitations that it had considered important to have clearly articulated, but it left much of the actual operating structure to be worked out on the basis of experience. For example, there is no mention of a "cabinet" in the Constitution, yet George Washington, the first president, convened the heads of the executive departments on a regular basis to advise him, and the Cabinet has become part of the American government.

One unique aspect of the American system has been the role played by the courts. Although the Constitution set up three branches of government - the legislative, executive and judicial - it devoted relatively little space to the role of the courts, assuming that judges would know what to do. But unlike Great Britain, where there was little interplay between the courts and the other branches of government, in the United States the Supreme Court has become a balance wheel of constitutional government. The Supreme Court is the final arbiter of what the Constitution means. In many of its decisions in the last two centuries the Court has arbitrated between the executive and legislative branches, and has also spelled out both the powers and the limits of the federal government.

Fledgling American Democracy (1789-1850)

From 1789 through 1850, the United States worked hard to establish itself as a distinguished democracy. During this period the wobbling thirteen states had grown into a strong nation of thirty-one states spanning from the Atlantic to the Pacific coast. The population increased to 23 million. The area of the United States had increased to 7.8 million square kilometers, almost tripled!

There were thirteen presidents up to this point – beginning with George Washington and ending with Millard Fillmore. In 1789 George Washington was elected as the first President of the United States. During his tenure the first ten amendments to the Constitution - the Bill of Rights - were created. In 1791, George Washington himself selected the site for the new capital of the country, which was fittingly named after him. The other Presidents who served during that time period were:

President	Important Events
1797-1800: John Adams	Washington refused a third term, at which point became an unbroken tradition untill 1940. Adams, a Federalist, lacked charisma and his "Alien and Sedition Acts" drew antagonism.
1801-1808: Thomas Jefferson	A Democrat, he is considered one of the chief architects of American Democracy. He added more territory." The principle of Judicial Review of legislation, "became a guiding principle and was an outcome of the Supreme Court's declaration of an act of Congress Unconstitutional. In 1807 The Congress halted the import of slaves into the U.S.

1809-1817: James Madison	Oversaw the War of 1812 against Britain, the War of 1815 at New Orleans and the "Treaty of Ghent."
1818-1823: James Monroe	His presidency was known as the "era of good feeling." More territories added, and to stop the European and South American interference, the "Monroe Doctrine" was proclaimed in 1823.
1824: John Quincy Adams	The House of Representatives named Adams as President as none of the contesting candidates recieved a majority of electoral votes.
1828-1835: Andrew Jackson	He was identified with the common people, and strengthened the Federal Government.
1836-1839: Martin Van Buren	His tenure saw a relentless depression. Whig Party was born.
1840: William Henry Harrison	The first Whig Party President, but with a short lived Presidency. He died after one month of assuming office.
1840: John Tyler	William Henry Harrison's Democaratic Vice-President. A milestone of his tenure is the Oregon Trail, and the foundation of railroads, telegraphs and canals. Texas annexed during his time.
1845: James Polk	The Mexican War started under his leadership; the treaty of Guadalupe-Hidalgo ended that war in 1848. New Mexico and California were ceded by Mexico as a result.
1849: Zachary Taylor	The second Whig President and hero of the Mexican War. He died very early in office.
1849: Millard Fillmore	He was caught in the web of the slavery issue. Congress passed the "Compromise of 1850, where California was made a free state. New Mexico and Utah, though, were slave states, and that fact was not mentioned.

Slavery, Fight for Equality, Civil War and Reunification

By 1850, the United States grew to house 23 million people. The total area grew to 7.8 million square kilometers. The vast expanse of the United States had varied climatic conditions, natural resources, a social fabric and industries and business. In legal matters, local affairs were ruled on by the States while matters of common interest were held by the federal Government. Sustained growth brought in its wake differences between States. The issue that was threatening the very fabric of the existence of the U.S. democracy itself was slavery. Slaves were used extensively in the cotton and tobacco plantations of the South. The North became critical of slave bonding. They talked about abolishing slavery to maintain human dignity. Those people were known as Abolitionists. The 'compromise of 1850' allayed the Southern fears temporarily. During the next ten years tension increased between the North and South on slavery, and the States rights to make their own rules regarding it.

In 1852, Franklin Pierce, a Democrat, became the 14th President. His "Kansas-Nebraska" Act of 1854 aroused passions and resulted in the formation of the Anti-Slavery Republican Party. The North, South divide reached a feverish pitch during the time of the 15th President's, Democrat James Buchanan, tenure largely because of the Supreme Court's Dred Scott Decision. The North was furious. In 1857 the raid on Harpers Ferry by John Brown alienated the South. In the late 1850s Minnesota, Oregon and Kansas - three Anti-Slavery States - were admitted to the United States. This rang loud alarm bells in the South!

In 1860, Abraham Lincoln, a Republican candidate, was elected President. The angered South took direct action. South Carolina, Mississippi, Florida, Alabama, Georgia, Louisiana and Texas seceded from the United States. They created a new Government of their own known as the "Confederate States of America."

Black Slavery, Agrarianism and Abolitionism

The Abolitionists were against slavery and worked hard to end it. When Quakers came to the new world, they protested slavery. By the 1770's there was a glut in the tobacco supplies. Tobacco merchants found it difficult to realize even the cost of production. The white landlords started to believe that the system of slavery should end. Northern states thought of a gradual abolition of slavery. Most black slaves were from Africa. American colonization society wanted the black slaves to be sent to Liberia in Africa. However, they did not succeed in sending many slaves.

During the 1830's, Radical abolitionists wanted an early end to slavery. Their leader William Lloyd Garrison demanded an end to slavery and giving equal rights to the blacks. He was to face the wrath of other whites. Some radical Abolitionists thought to enter politics to end slavery.

The Liberty Party was born which in the course of time became the Free Soil Party and ultimately the Republican Party. Immediately after the American Civil War, the fifteenth Amendment to the constitution was passed abolishing slavery.

Those who supported agrarianism believed in a society full of independent landed farmers. They believed in rural strengths and abhorred cities. To them, industries beget corruption and slowly turn the whole fabric of the society into an immoral one. Thomas Jefferson as well as many Republicans subscribed to this view. The industrial revolution and the exponential growth of infra-structure and cities dealt a deathblow to agrarianism.

Introduction to the Court Opinion on the Dred Scott Case

Dred Scott's case holds a unique place in American constitutional history as an example of the Supreme Court trying to impose a judicial solution on a political problem. It called down enormous criticism on the Court and on Chief Justice Roger Brooke Taney; a later chief justice, Charles Evans Hughes, described it as a great "self-inflicted wound."

Scott, born a slave, had been taken by his master, an army surgeon, into the free portion of the Louisiana territory. Upon his master's death, Scott sued for his freedom, on the grounds that since slavery was outlawed in the free territory, he had become a free man there, and "once free always free." The argument was rejected by a Missouri court, but Scott and his white supporters managed to get the case into federal court, where the issue was simply whether a slave had standing -- that is, the legal right -- to sue in a federal court. So the first question the Supreme Court had to decide was whether it had jurisdiction. If Scott had standing, then the Court had jurisdiction, and the justices could go on to decide the merits of his claim. But if, as a slave, Scott did not have standing, then the Court could dismiss the suit for lack of jurisdiction.

The Court ruled that Scott, as a slave, could not exercise the prerogative of a free citizen to sue in federal court. That should have been the end of the case, but Chief Justice Taney and the other southern sympathizers on the Court hoped that a definitive ruling would settle the issue of slavery in the territories once and for all. So they went on to rule that the Missouri Compromise of 1820 was unconstitutional since Congress could not forbid citizens from taking their property, i.e., slaves, into any territory owned by the United States. A slave, Taney ruled, was property, nothing more, and could never be a citizen.

The South, of course, welcomed the ruling, but in the North it raised a storm of protest and scorn. It helped create the Republican Party, and disgust at the decision may have played a role in the election of Abraham Lincoln in 1860.

Dred Scott v. Sandford (1857)

Chief Justice Taney delivered the opinion of the Court:

"The question is simply this: Can a negro, whose ancestors were imported into this country, and sold as slaves, become a member of the political community formed and brought into existence by the Constitution of the United States, and as such become entitled to all the rights, and privileges, and immunities, guaranteed by that instrument to the citizen? One of which rights is the privilege of suing in a court of the United States in the cases specified in the constitution...

"The words "people of the United States" and "citizens" are synonymous terms, and mean the same thing. They both describe the political body who, according to our republican institutions, form the sovereignty, and who hold the power and conduct the government through their representatives. They are what we familiarly call the "sovereign people," and every citizen is one of this people, and a constituent member of this sovereignty. The question before us is, whether the class of persons described in the plea in abatement compose a portion of this people, and are constituent members of this sovereignty? We think they are not, and that they are not included, and were not intended to be included, under the word "citizens" in the constitution, and can therefore claim none of the rights and privileges which that instrument provides for and secures to citizens of the United States. On the contrary, they were at that time considered as a subordinate and inferior class of beings, who had been subjugated by the dominant race, and, whether emancipated or not, yet remained subject to their authority, and had no rights or privileges but such as those who held the power and the government might choose to grant them.

"It is not the province of the court to decide upon the justice or injustice, the policy or impolicy, of these laws. The decision of that question belonged to the political or law-making power; to those who formed the sovereignty and framed the constitution. The duty of the court is, to interpret the instrument they have framed, with the best lights we can obtain on the subject, and to administer it as we find it, according to its true intent and meaning when it was adopted.

"In discussing this question, we must not confound the rights of citizenship which a State may confer within its own limits, and the rights of citizenship as a member of the Union. It does not by any means follow, because he has all the rights and privileges of a citizen of a State, that he must be a citizen of the United States. He may have all of the rights and privileges of the citizen of a State, and yet not be entitled to the rights and privileges of a citizen in any other State. For, previous to the adoption of the constitution of the United States, every State had the undoubted right to confer on whomsoever it pleased the character of citizen, and to endow him with all its rights. But this character of course was confirmed to the boundaries of the State, and gave him no rights or privileges in other States beyond those secured to him by the laws of nations and the comity of States. Nor have the several States surrendered the power of conferring these rights and privileges by adopting the constitution of the United States...

"It is very clear, therefore, that no State can, by any act or law of its own, passed since the adoption of the constitution, introduce a new member into the political community created by the constitution of the United States. It cannot make him a member of this community by making him a member of its own. And for the same reason it cannot introduce any person, or description of persons, who were not intended to be embraced in this new political family, which the constitution brought into existence, but were intended to be excluded from it.

"The question then arises, whether the provisions of the constitution, in relation to the personal rights and privileges to which the citizen of a State should be entitled, embraced the negro African race, at that time in this country, or who might afterwards be imported, who had then or should afterwards be made free in any State; and to put it in the power of a single State to make him a citizen of the United States, and endue him with the full rights of citizenship in every other State without their consent? Does the constitution of the United States act upon him whenever he shall be made free under the laws of a State, and raised there to the rank of a citizen, and immediately clothe him with all the privileges of a citizen in every other State, and in its own courts?

"The court think the affirmative of these propositions cannot be maintained. And if it cannot, the plaintiff in error could not be a citizen of the State of Missouri, within the meaning of the constitution of the United States, and, consequently, was not entitled to sue in its courts.

"It is true, every person, and every class and description of persons, who were at the time of the adoption of the constitution recognized as citizens in the several States, became also citizens of this new political body; but none other; it was formed by them, and for them and their posterity, but for no one else. And the personal rights and privileges guaranteed to citizens of this new sovereignty were intended to embrace those only who were then members of the several State communities, or who should afterwards by birthright or otherwise become members, according to the provisions of the constitution and the principles on which it was founded. It was the union of those who were at that time members of distinct and separate political communities into one political family, whose power, for certain specified purposes, was to extend over the whole territory of the United States. And it gave to each citizen rights and privileges outside of his State which he did not before possess, and placed him in every other State upon a perfect equality with its own citizens as to rights of person and rights of property; it made him a citizen of the United States...

"In the opinion of the court, the legislation and histories of the times, and the language used in the declaration of independence, show, that neither the class of persons who had been imported as slaves, nor their descendants, whether they had become free or not, were then acknowledged as a part of the people, nor intended to be included in the general words used in that memorable instrument...

"It is too clear for dispute, that the enslaved African race were not intended to be included, and formed no part of the people who framed and adopted this declaration; for if the language, as understood in that day, would embrace them, the conduct of the distinguished men who framed the declaration of independence would have been utterly and flagrantly inconsistent with the principles they asserted; and instead of the sympathy of mankind, to which they so confidently appealed, they would have deserved and received universal rebuke and reprobation...

"But there are two clauses in the constitution which point directly and specifically to the negro race as a separate class of persons, and show clearly that they were not regarded as a portion of the people or citizens of the government then formed.

"One of these clauses reserves to each of the thirteen States the right to import slaves until the year 1808, if it thinks proper...And by the other provision the States pledge themselves to each other to maintain the right of property of the master, by delivering up to him any slave who may have escaped from his service, and be found within their respective territories...

"The only two provisions which point to them and include them, treat them as property, and make it the duty of the government to protect it; no other power, in relation to this race, is to be found in the constitution; and as it is a government of special, delegated powers, no authority beyond these two provisions can be constitutionally exercised.

The government of the United States had no right to interfere for any other purpose but that of protecting the rights of the owner, leaving it altogether with the several States to deal with this race, whether emancipated or not, as each State may think justice, humanity, and the interests and safety of society, require. The States evidently intended to reserve this power exclusively to themselves...

"Upon a full and careful consideration of the subject, the court is of opinion, that, upon the facts stated...Dred Scott was not a citizen of Missouri within the meaning of the constitution of the United States, and not entitled as such to sue in its courts; and, consequently, that the circuit court had no jurisdiction of the case, and that the judgment on the plea in abatement is erroneous...

"We proceed...to inquire whether the facts relied on by the plaintiff entitled him to his freedom...

"The act of Congress, upon which the plaintiff relies, declares that slavery and involuntary servitude, except as a punishment for crime, shall be forever prohibited in all that part of the territory ceded by France, under the name of Louisiana, which lies north of thirty-six degrees thirty minutes north latitude and not included within the limits of Missouri. And the difficulty which meets us at the threshold of this part of the inquiry is whether Congress was authorized to pass this law under any of the powers granted to it by the Constitution; for, if the authority is not given by that instrument, it is the duty of this Court to declare it void and inoperative and incapable of conferring freedom upon anyone who is held as a slave under the laws of any one of the states.

"The counsel for the plaintiff has laid much stress upon that article in the Constitution which confers on Congress the power "to dispose of and make all needful rules and regulations respecting the territory or other property belonging to the United States"; but, in the judgment of the Court, that provision has no bearing on the present controversy, and the power there given, whatever it may be, is confined, and was intended to be confined, to the territory which at that time belonged to, or was claimed by, the United States and was within their boundaries as settled by the treaty with Great Britain and can have no influence upon a territory afterward acquired from a foreign government. It was a special provision for a known and particular territory, and to meet a present emergency, and nothing more...

"We do not mean, however, to question the power of Congress in this respect. The power to expand the territory of the United States by the admission of new states is plainly given; and in the construction of this power by all the departments of the government, it has been held to authorize the acquisition of territory, not fit for admission at the time, but to be admitted as soon as its population and situation would entitle it to admission...

"It may be safely assumed that citizens of the United States who migrate to a territory belonging to the people of the United States cannot be ruled as mere colonists, dependent upon the will of the general government, and to be governed by any laws it may think proper to impose. The principle upon which our governments rest, and upon which alone they continue to exist, is the union of states, sovereign and independent within their own limits in their internal and domestic concerns, and bound together as one people by a general government, possessing certain enumerated and restricted powers, delegated to it by the people of the several states, and exercising supreme authority within the scope of the powers granted to it, throughout the dominion of the United States. A power, therefore, in the general government to obtain and hold colonies and dependent territories, over which they might legislate without restriction, would be inconsistent with its own existence in its present form. Whatever it acquires, it acquires for the benefit of the people of the several states who created it. It is their trustee acting for them and charged with the duty of promoting the interests of the whole people of the Union in the exercise of the powers specifically granted...

"But the power of Congress over the person or property of a citizen can never be a mere discretionary power under our Constitution and form of government. The powers of the government and the rights and privileges of the citizen are regulated and plainly defined by the Constitution itself. And, when the territory becomes a part of the United States, the federal government enters into possession in the character impressed upon it by those who created it. It enters upon it with its powers over the citizen strictly defined and limited by the Constitution, from which it derives its own existence, and by virtue of which alone it continues to exist and act as a government and sovereignty. It has no power of any kind beyond it; and it cannot, when it enters a territory of the United States, put off its character and assume discretionary or despotic powers which the Constitution has denied to it. It cannot create for itself a new character separated from the citizens of the United States and the duties it owes them under the provisions of the Constitution. The territory, being a part of the United States, the government and the citizen both enter it under the authority of the Constitution, with their respective rights defined and marked out; and the federal government can exercise no power over his person or property, beyond what that instrument confers, nor lawfully deny any right which it has reserved...

"These powers, and others, in relation to rights of person, which it is not necessary here to enumerate, are, in express and positive terms, denied to the general government; and the rights of private property have been guarded with equal care. Thus the rights of property are united with the rights of person and placed on the same ground by the Fifth Amendment to the Constitution, which provides that no person shall be deprived of life, liberty, and property without due process of law. And an act of Congress which deprives a citizen of the United States of his liberty or property, without due process of law, merely because he came himself or brought his property into a particular territory of the United States, and who had committed no offense against the laws, could hardly be dignified with the name of due process of law...

"It seems, however, to be supposed that there is a difference between property in a slave and other property and that different rules may be applied to it in expounding the Constitution of the United States. And the laws and usages of nations, and the writings of eminent jurists upon the relation of master and slave and their mutual rights and duties, and the powers which governments may exercise over it, have been dwelt upon in the argument.

"But, in considering the question before us, it must be borne in mind that there is no law of nations standing between the people of the United States and their government and interfering with their relation to each other. The powers of the government and the rights of the citizen under it are positive and practical regulations plainly written down. The people of the United States have delegated to it certain enumerated powers and forbidden it to exercise others. It has no power over the person or property of a citizen but what the citizens of the United States have granted. And no laws or usages of other nations, or reasoning of statesmen or jurists upon the relations of master and slave, can enlarge the powers of the government or take from the citizens the rights they have reserved. And if the Constitution recognizes the right of property of the master in a slave, and makes no distinction between that description of property and other property owned by a citizen, no tribunal, acting under the authority of the United States, whether it be legislative, executive, or judicial, has a right to draw such a distinction or deny to it the benefit of the provisions and guaranties which have been provided for the protection of private property against the encroachments of the government.

"Now, as we have already said in an earlier part of this opinion, upon a different point, the right of property in a slave is distinctly and expressly affirmed in the Constitution. The right to traffic in it, like an ordinary article of merchandise and property, was guaranteed to the citizens of the United States, in every state that might desire it, for twenty years. And the government in express terms is pledged to protect it in all future time if the slave escapes from his owner. That is done in plain words -- too plain to be misunderstood. And no word can be found in the Constitution which gives Congress a greater power over slave property or which entitles property of that kind to less protection than property of any other description. The only power conferred is the power coupled with the duty of guarding and protecting the owner in his rights.

"Upon these considerations it is the opinion of the Court that the act of Congress which prohibited a citizen from holding and owning property of this kind in the territory of the United States north of the line therein mentioned is not warranted by the Constitution and is therefore void; and that neither Dred Scott himself, nor any of his family, were made free by being carried into this territory; even if they had been carried there by the owner with the intention of becoming a permanent resident.

# The American Civil War

Confederate forces fired on the Union-held Fort Sumter on April 12, 1861. This act was seen as a rebellion by President Lincoln. He responded by drafting 75,000 volunteers for military service. Four Southern States - North Carolina, Arkansas, Virginia and Tennessee - enraged by this action, seceded from the Union. There erupted a major battle in July 1861 between Confederate forces and the Union army at Bull Run (Manassas). The war went into many fronts, one by one, during the years between 1861 and 1865. Gen. Ulysses S. Grant fought and won many battles and, finally, the war for the Union.

With the surrender of Gen. Joseph Johnston's Confederate troops in Durham, N.C. on April 26, 1865 the Union Government scored a decisive win over the war. During the war, West Virginia and Nevada were added to the Union. In 1864 Lincoln was re-elected but to the great dismay of the nation and the world, he was assassinated within a month. Andrew Johnson, Lincoln's Vice-President became President. During his tenure, the 13th and 14th Amendments abolished Slavery and granted Civil Rights for all.

Nebraska joined the Union in 1867 and Alaska was purchased from Russia. In 1868, Ulysses S. Grant, the Civil War hero, became the Republican President. Black Americans were given the right to vote by the 15th Amendment to the constitution. The 38th State, in the form of Colorado, joined the Union. With Grant's exit in 1877, the depression was also over.

# Political Institutions, Political Developments, Behavior and Public Policy

In 1619 the London Company gave a share in the government to the settlers. In each settlement men were allowed to elect two of their own kith and kin to represent them in the Government. They used to attend meetings called by the Colonial Governor in Jamestown to enact laws. This was the first ever democratic setup in America. It happened in the very first colony -Virginia in the year 1619 itself and had become a model for others to follow.

On the 20th of November, the Pilgrims made a solemn promise to each other before their feet touched the sands of Provincetown. They promised to obey all laws, rules and regulations that they themselves would adopt. This became the famous "Mayflower

Compact Agreement." This is a great step taken by the Pilgrims towards democracy and self-governance.

The Puritan leaders held a tight grip on governance. Protests started and finally the leaders gave the right to vote to all Puritan men. Every town was allowed to govern itself. At the town meetings citizens decided on issues and voted. Majority vote won the decision. In the Massachusetts Bay colony also, as in Virginia, settlers believed in the form of a democratic self-governance.

Rhode Island, in fact, became a model of freedom. Every citizen had freedom of speech. People were allowed to worship as they pleased. Everyone had a vote and more importantly, they had the right to hold public office.

In 1649, the Maryland legislature adopted a law that became known as the "Toleration Act" which ensured religious freedom to all Christians who settled in the colony of Maryland.

From 1619 through the next 150 plus years, the colonies developed their own society, value systems, economy, and attempts at a democratic form of self-governance. There was no interference from England. However, after the Paris Treaty of 1763, there was a perceptible change in the behavior of England towards the American colonies.

The first ever attempt to unite the colonies was ideated by Benjamin Franklin in 1754. The plan was adopted by the Albany Congress but was rejected by both Britain and the colonies.

At the birth of the nation in 1776, ninety percent of the American people were farmers.

The first Government of the New States of America was an informal one. The colonies had sent people to represent their colony to a Continental Congress, which met in the year 1744 and again in 1775 in Philadelphia. The idea was to get greater freedom from Parliamentary rule. The same Continental Congress declared independence in the year 1776.

The Continental Congress was a temporary arrangement. In 1781, the States decided to form the Government of the United States of America. This would be a Congress to which each and every State sent delegates. The States retained the power to recall any delegate if his conduct was not satisfactory in the Congress. Each State had one Vote in the Congress irrespective of the number of delegates it sent to the Congress. For a law to be passed, nine out of thirteen States had to agree. The Congress had powers to mint coins, borrow money, operate post offices, raise armies, sign treaties etc. These powers were clearly written in black and white. That document was known as the "Articles of Confederation." In fact the Government of United States of America was known as a confederation. The confederation was in force for eight years. The beauty of the confederation was that though it firmly put in place a Central Government, it did not dilute the powers enjoyed by the States in any way. Additionally, the citizens had a State Government of their own. And, importantly, in the history of the world, there was a written document - a constitution - for the United States. No other country had this sort of written arrangement.

People who wanted a strong central Government with supreme powers were known as the Federalists. Chief among them was George Washington. In order to strengthen the Government under the Articles, the Federalists called a Constitutional Convention that met in Philadelphia in the year 1787, with only Rhode Island absent. They, after due deliberations, brought in a new constitution. It was this document, approved by the States that replaced the articles in the year 1789.

The Congress of the United States is the Law making body of the Federal Government in Washington; DC.

The Federalist Party enacted alien and sedition laws, which became very unpopular.

Thomas Jefferson's Democratic-Republican Party was renamed the Democratic Party.

During Martin Van Buren's Presidency, the great depression continued relentlessly. This paved the way for the "Whig Party" to come into being.

President Franklin Pierce's "Kansas-Nebraska" Act of 1854 aroused passions and resulted in the formation of the anti-slavery "Republican Party."

Years of political wisdom made the people of the United States wiser. They had had enough of having many parties. They came to the conclusion that two strong national Parties could only benefit them in the long run. The result was a two party system consisting of a Democratic Party and Republican Party.

The Content of the Constitution

The Constitution guarantees the rights and liberties of the people. It is the supreme law of the land. The principle of "Separation of Powers" is adhered to according to each wing of the government - the legislative, the executive and the judiciary – and they do maintain their separate identity. Section 8 of Article I of the Constitution dictates what congress shall do. These powers are known as delegated powers. Other than those, anything else the state government shall want to do is left to the states. These are residual powers. Taxing shall be exercised by both state and federal government. Such powers are known as concurrent powers.

The Constitution of the United States of America consists of:

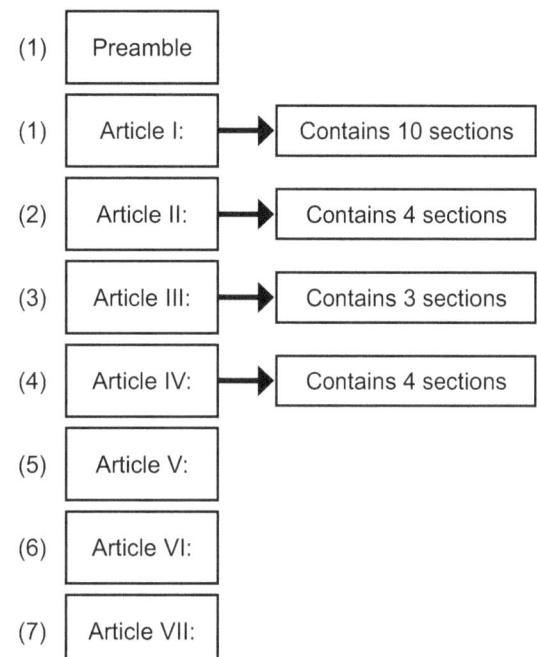

A dynamic constitution has to change with the times - this is made possible by bringing in amendments to the constitution. Originally, there were ten amendments to the constitution of United States of America (December 15, 1791).

 The Ten Original Amendments

AMENDMENT 1

Congress shall make no law respecting an establishment of religion, or prohibiting the free exercise thereof; or abridging the freedom of speech, or of the press; or the right of the people peaceably to assemble, and to petition the government for a redress of grievances.

AMENDMENT 2

A well-regulated Militia, being necessary to the security of a free state, the right of the people to keep and bear Arms, shall not be infringed.

AMENDMENT 3

No Soldier shall, in time of peace be quartered in any house, without the consent of the Owner, nor in time of war, but in manner to be prescribed by law.

AMENDMENT 4

The right of the people to be secure in their persons, house, papers, and effects, against unreasonable searches and seizures, shall not be violated, and no Warrants shall issue, but upon probable cause, supported by Oath or affirmation, and particularly describing the place to be searched, and the persons or things to be seized.

AMENDMENT 5

No person shall be held to answer for a capital, or otherwise infamous crime, unless on a presentment or indictment of a Grand Jury, except in cases arising in the land or naval forces, or in the Militia, when in actual service in time of War or public danger; nor shall any person be subject for the same offense to be twice put in jeopardy of life or limb; nor shall be compelled in any criminal case to be a witness against himself, nor be deprived of life, liberty, or property, without due process of law; nor shall private property be taken for public use, without just compensation.

AMENDMENT 6

In all criminal prosecutions, the accused shall enjoy the right to a speedy and public trial, by an impartial jury of the State and district where in the crime shall have been committed, which district shall have been previously ascertained by law, and to be informed of nature and cause of the accusation; to be confronted with the witnesses against him; to have compulsory process for obtaining witnesses in his favor, and to have the Assistance of Counsel for his defense.

AMENDMENT 7

In suits at common law, where the value in controversy shall exceed twenty dollars, the right of trial by a jury shall be otherwise re-examined in any Court of the United States, than according to the rules of the common law.

AMENDMENT 8

Excessive bail shall not be required, nor excessive fines imposed, nor cruel and unusual punishments inflicted.

AMENDMENT 9

The enumeration in the Constitution, of certain rights, shall not be construed to deny or disparage others retained by the people.

AMENDMENT 10

The powers not delegated to the United States by the Constitution, nor prohibited by it to the States, are reserved to the State respectively, or to the people.

AMENDMENT 13, RATIFIED IN 1865

Section 1: Neither slavery nor involuntary servitude except as a punishment for crime whereof the party shall have been duly convicted shall exist within the United States, nor any place subject to their jurisdiction.

Section 2: Congress shall have power to enforce this article by appropriate legislation.

AMENDMENT 15, RATIFIED IN 1870

Section 1: The right of citizens of the United States to vote shall not be denied or abridged by the United States or by any State on account of race, color, or previous condition of servitude.

Section 2: The Congress shall have power to enforce this article by appropriate legislation.

AMENDMENT 19, RATIFIED IN 1920

The right of citizens of the United States to vote shall not be denied or abridged by the United States or by any States on account of sex. The Congress shall have power to enforce this article by appropriate legislation.

AMENDMENT 26, RATIFIED IN 1971

Section 1: The right of citizens of the United States, who are 18 years of age or older, to vote shall not be denied or abridged by the United States or any state on account of age.

Section 2: The Congress shall have the power to enforce this article by appropriate legislation.

How to Make Amendments to the Constitution

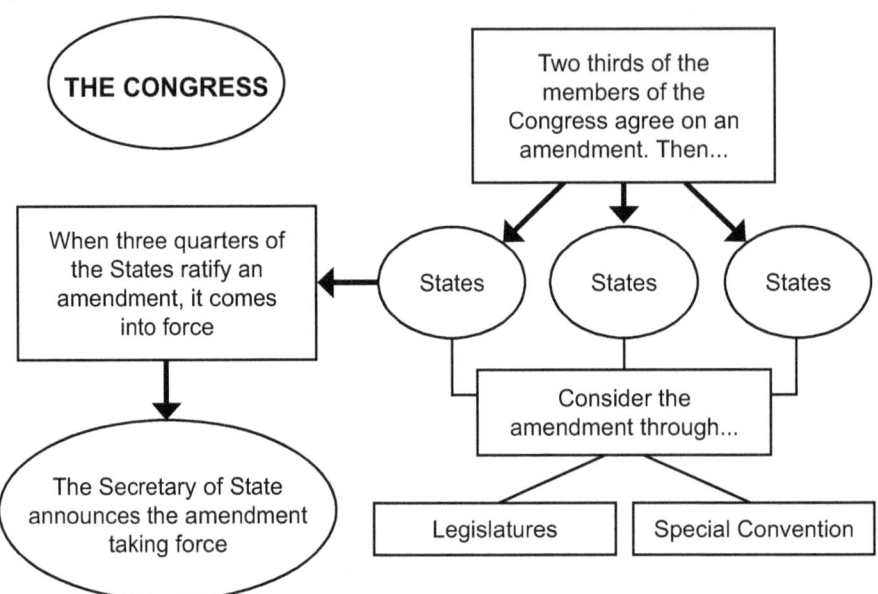

The Supreme Court also interprets the constitution the way it deems fit and just. The first ever judicial review came in 1803 in the case of Marbury vs. Madison in which the Supreme Court declared an act of the Congress unconstitutional.

IMPORTANT LEGAL ACTS PASSED DURING 1770 TO 1887 AD

1. The Alien and Sedition Acts of 1798:

Jeffersonian Republicans were of the view that the raging revolution in France at that time was good for the people and welcomed it. However, the Federalists thought it was not good from the U.S. standpoint. The Federalists were in total control of the Congress and passed two Acts, which were, on the surface of it, aimed at safeguarding the Nation from the perceived threat from the French. They were: (1) The Naturalization Act and, (2) The Alien and Sedition Acts. In reality, the acts were pointed at the Republican opposition. There was also an undercurrent of opinion which felt that the aliens living in the states could take sides and support the French, if a war broke out. During wartime all aliens could be deported or arrested and put in prison during the course of a war. The Naturalization Act increased the residential status of five years for citizenship to 14 years. The Sedition Act spelled out that anyone who indulged in writing or speaking against the Congress, or the President, with "intent to defame" or bring either to contempt, was to be considered as a criminal offender. People who were charged with the Acts were invariably Republicans and the judges, Federalists. Mercifully, all these Acts were allowed to expire in 1800 and 1801 when Republicans came to power.

2. The Northwest Ordinance of 1787:

It is still considered one of the most exceptional pieces of legislation ever enacted in the U.S. The ordinance stipulated that all new states to be created north of the Ohio River would enjoy the same legal status as the existing states. Slavery was excluded from the area. This ordinance in essence was a sort of "elastic federalism" that paved the way for further opening up the American continent and extending the Union.

3. The Kansas-Nebraska Act in 1854:

During the Presidency of Franklin Pierce, a Democrat from New Hampshire, the Kansas-Nebraska Act was passed in 1854. The result: (1) It sped up the organization of the anti-slavery party - The Republican Party, (2) The rift between the slavery-nurturing South and the anti-slavery North became very wide, and (3) It slowly but surely drove the South and North towards war - The Civil War.

4. The Pacific Railway Acts, 1862:

It specified the Thirty-Second parallel as the first transcontinental route. It also provided enormous chunks of lands as grants for paving the railroad. The Act also authorized (1) The Central Pacific and (2) The Union Pacific railroad companies to pave railway lines.

5. General Allotment Act, 1887 (a.k.a. Dawes Act, 1887):

Senator Henry Dawes of Massachusetts brought in this legislation to Congress which passed it on February 8, 1887. It is "an act to provide for the Allotment of Lands in severalty to Indians on the various reservations." The importance of this legislation was to decree that Native Americans would be treated not as members of various tribes but as individuals and allot them land. A reservation land held by members of a clan or tribe severally could be broken up and distributed to an individual by a Presidential order. According to the Act, the land provision would be: (a) head of families - 120 acres, (b) each single person over 18 years of age, or, orphan child under age 18 - 60 acres and, (c) any other single individual under age 18 - 30 acres. However, this act did not apply to territories belonging to: (1) Cherokees, (2) Creeks, (3) Choctaws, (4) Chickasaws, (5) Osage (6) Seminoles (7) Sacs and Foxes, (8) Miamis and Peorias.

Founding Fathers

Why are they called Founding Fathers? What did they do? The term "Founding Fathers" tells us not what they dreamt but actually what they did. They became the fathers of the United States of America, through their actions. Who are they? There are still raging arguments on who should be included in the history books of the U.S.A as Founding Fathers. However, there is a modicum of consensus to include (1) those statesmen who toiled to secure independence from the British Empire, and (2) those who used their brains in shaping the most brilliant and workable document - The Constitution of the United States of America, which is still relevant even after 200 years.

We know that the first Government of the New States of America was an informal one. The colonies had sent representatives to a Continental Congress, which met in the year 1744 and again in 1775 in Philadelphia. The idea was to wrest greater freedom from Parliamentary rule. The same Continental Congress declared independence in the year 1776. On July 4, 1776, the Congress adopted one of the most famous documents in the United States history, prepared by Thomas Jefferson, *The Declaration of Independence.*

The Constitution resembled the articles in many respects. There were two governments - the National/Federal, and the States. However, the Central Government of the United States of America could make laws that had to be obeyed by all the people in all the States. A chief executive, who was elected by the people of the United States, was vested with exceptional powers. This made the form of government a Republic - no hereditary King, at the helm of affairs, but an elected executive. The constitution made the congress representatives of the people on the one hand and the States on the other. The Government that under the articles was "of the States, by the States and for the States" had indeed become a government "of the people, by the people and for the people." Americans have lived with the same Constitution for over 200 years now, which is unique. Of course, there were many amendments to the constitution. Over the years, the Supreme Court has provided interpretations to the Constitution, giving new meaning to the original words.

Given below are the names of people who signed the Declaration of Independence and are also considered Founding Fathers of United States of America.

Massachusetts	Connecticut	Pennsylvania	Maryland	North Carolina
John Hancock	Roger Sherman	Robert Morris	Samuel Chase	William Hooper
Samuel Adams	Samuel Huntington	Benjamin Rush	William Paca	Joseph Hewes
John Adams	William Williams	Benjamin Franklin	Thomas Stone	John Penn
Robert Treat Paine	Oliver Wolcott	John Morton	Charles Carrol	
Elbridge Gerry		George Clymer		**South Carolina**
	New York	James Smith	**Virginia**	Edward Rutledge
New Hampshire	William Floyd	George Taylor	George Wythe	Thomas Heyward
Josiah Bartlett	Philip Livingston	James Wilson	Richard Henry Lee	Thomas Lynch
William Whipple	Francis Lewis	George Ross	Thomas Jefferson	Arthur Middleton
Matthew Thornton	Lewis Morris		Benjamin Harrison	
		Delaware	Thomas Nelson, Jr.	**Georgia**
Rhode Island	**New Jersey**	Caesar Rodney	Francis Lightfoot Lee	Button Gwinnett
Stephen Hopkins	Richard Stockton	George Read	Carter Braxton	Lyman Hall
William Ellery	John Witherspoon	Thomas M'Kean		George Walton
	Francis Hopkinson			
	John Hart			
	Abraham Clark			

Then, there were the signers of the Articles of Confederation.

New Hampshire	Connecticut	Pennsylvania	Maryland	North Carolina
Josiah Bartlett	Roger Sherman	Robert Morris	John Hanson	John Penn
John Wentworth, Jr.	Samuel Huntington	Daniel Roberdeau	Daniel Carroll	Henry Laurens
	Oliver Wolcott	Jonathan Bayard		William Henry
Massachusetts	Titus Hosmer	Smith	**Virginia**	Drayton
John Hancock	Andrew Adams	William Clingan	Richard Henry Lee	John Mathews
Samuel Adams		Joseph Reed	John Banister	Richard Hutson
Elbridge Gerry	**New York**		Thomas Adams	Thomas Heyward, Jr.
Francis Dana	James Duane	**Delaware**	John Harvie	
James Lovell	Francis Lewis	Thomas McKean	Francis Lightfoot	**Georgia**
Samuel Holten	William Duer	John Dickinson	Lee	John Walton
	Gouverneur Morris	Nicholas Van Dyke		Edward Telfair
Rhode Island				Edward Langworthy
William Ellery	**New Jersey**			
Henry Marchant	John Witherspoon			
John Collins	Nathaniel Scudder			

And, finally, there were people who took an active part in the deliberations that fashioned the document known as The Constitution of the United States of America. The signers were:

New Hampshire John Langdon Nicholas Gilman **Massachusetts** Rufus King Nathaniel Gorham **Connecticut** Roger Sherman William Samuel Johnson **New York** Alexander Hamilton **New Jersey** William Livingston David Brearley William Paterson Jonathan Dayton	**Pennsylvania** Benjamin Franklin Thomas Mifflin Robert Morris George Clymer Thomas FitzSimons Jared Ingersoll Gouverneur Morris James Wilson **Delaware** George Read Gunning Bedford, Jr. John Dickinson Richard Bassett Jacob Broom **Maryland** James McHenry Daniel Carroll Dan of St. Thomas Jenifer	**Virginia** John Blair James Madison, Jr. George Washington **North Carolina** William Blount Richard Dobbs Spaight Hugh Williamson **South Carolina** John Rutledge Charles Cotesworth Pinckney Charles Pinckney Pierce Butler **Georgia** William Few Abraham Baldwin

Thirty-nine statesmen signed the Constitution in 1787. Some of the important statesmen like Jefferson and John Adams did not sign the document as they were in Europe when the Constitutional Convention was in session. There were seventy-four Founding Fathers appointed as delegates to the Constitutional Convention at Philadelphia in the year 1787, of which only fifty-five actually attended.

There were well-known statesmen founding fathers, like George Washington, Alexander Hamilton, Thomas Jefferson, Benjamin Franklin, James Madison, and John Adams. Two documents written by the Founding Fathers stand out. One is the Declaration of Independence and the other is The Constitution, with its Bill of Rights. These documents, even after a time lapse of 200 years, remain the most imitated, most quoted, and most discussed in the world.

Founding Fathers came from different backgrounds. A vast majority of them were highly educated men. During colonial times, there were only a very few schools available. It is, therefore, all the more striking that they educated themselves by utilizing whatever material was available, a most laudable feat indeed. A good many of them were not only trained in law but were in constant touch with the political philosophers of the day.

They had confidence in their own decisions and purpose in their deeds. They lived in a time when tremendous intellectual activity started to blossom. It was the "Age of Enlightenment." Science was just around the corner. Land in the American colonies was very cheap, which emphasized the philosophy of individual freedom and liberty. Those were the days when a settler could provide for himself and his family without any assistance from others.

The Founding Fathers believed in their people. They were of the opinion that the Americans had the capability not only to control their own destiny but to control nature as well for the overall good of humanity. They had an onerous task to perform, which many critics thought was impossible. Any lesser mortal would have given up, but they persevered. By resolve of hardwork and tenacity of purpose, they achieved their objectives. They mastered International Politics. All along they were certain that they could not fight the force of a mighty Empire alone. In 1776, Benjamin Franklin, a renowned orator and an exceptional negotiator, was sent to France as a Minister. He was instrumental in convincing the French to fight with the Colonists against the British Empire.

George Washington's Farewell Address

Friends and Fellow-Citizens:

The period for a new election of a citizen to administer the Executive Government of the United States being not far distant, and the time actually arrived when your thoughts must be employed in designating the person who is to be clothed with that important trust, it appears to me proper, especially as it may conduce to a more distinct expression of the public voice, that I should now apprise you of the resolution I have formed to decline being considered among the number of those out of whom a choice is to be made....

The impressions with which I first undertook the arduous trust were explained on the proper occasion. In the discharge of this trust I will only say that I have, with good intentions, contributed toward the organization and administration of the Government the best exertions of which a very fallible judgment was capable. Not unconscious in the outset of the inferiority of my qualifications, experience in my own eyes, perhaps still more in the eyes of others, has strengthened the motives to diffidence of myself; and every day the increasing weight of years admonishes me more and more that the shade of retirement is as necessary to me as it will be welcome. Satisfied that if any circumstances have given peculiar value to my services they were temporary, I have the consolation to believe that, while choice and prudence invite me to quit the political scene, patriotism does not forbid it....

Here, perhaps, I ought to stop. But a solicitude for your welfare which can not end with my life, and the apprehension of danger natural to that solicitude, urge me on an occasion like the present to offer to your solemn contemplation and to recommend to your frequent review some sentiments which are the result of much reflection, of no inconsiderable observation, and which appear to me all important to permanency of your felicity as a people.... Interwoven as is the love of liberty with every ligament of your hearts, no recommendation of mine is necessary to fortify or confirm the attachment.

The unity of government which constitutes you one people is also now dear to you. It is justly so, for it is a main pillar in the edifice of your real independence, the support of your tranquility at home, your peace abroad, of your safety, of your prosperity, of that very liberty which you so highly prize. But as it is easy to foresee that from different causes and from different quarters much pains will be taken, many artifices employed, to weaken in your minds the conviction of this truth, as this is the point in your political fortress against which the batteries of internal and external enemies will be most constantly and actively (though often covertly and insidiously) directed, it is of infinite moment that you should properly estimate the immense value of your national union to your collective and individual happiness; that you should cherish a cordial, habitual, and immovable attachment to it; accustoming yourselves to think and speak of it as of the palladium of your political safety and prosperity; watching for its preservation with jealous anxiety; discountenancing whatever may suggest even a suspicion that it can in any event be abandoned, and indignantly frowning upon the first dawning of every attempt to alienate any portion of our country from the rest or to enfeeble the sacred ties which now link together the various parts.

For this you have every inducement of sympathy and interest. Citizens by birth or choice of a common country, that country has a right to concentrate your affections. The name of American, which belongs to you in your national capacity, must always exalt the just pride of patriotism more than any appellation derived from local discriminations. With slight shades of difference, you have the same religion, manners, habits, and political principles. You have in a common cause fought and triumphed together. The independence and liberty you possess are the work of joint councils and joint efforts, of common dangers, sufferings, and successes.

But these considerations, however powerfully they address themselves to your sensibility, are greatly outweighed by those which apply more immediately to your interest. Here every portion of our country finds the most commanding motives for carefully guarding and preserving the union of the whole.

The North, in an unrestrained intercourse with the South, protected by the equal laws of a common government, finds in the productions of the latter great additional resources of maritime and commercial enterprise and precious materials of manufacturing industry. The South, in the same intercourse, benefiting by the same agency of the North, sees its agriculture grow and its commerce expand. Turning partly into its own channels the seamen of the North, it finds its particular navigation invigorated; and while it contributes in different ways to nourish and increase the general mass of the national navigation, it looks forward to the protection of a maritime strength to which itself is unequally adapted. The East, in a like intercourse with the West, already finds, and in the progressive improvement of interior communications by land and water will more and more find, a valuable vent for the commodities which it brings from abroad or manufactures at home. The West derives from the East supplies requisite to its growth and comfort, and what is perhaps of still greater consequence, it must of necessity owe the secure enjoyment of indispensable outlets for its own productions to the weight, influence, and the future maritime strength of the Atlantic side of the Union, directed by an indissoluble community of interest as one nation. Any other tenure by which the West can hold this essential advantage, whether derived from its own separate strength or from an apostate and unnatural connection with any foreign power, must be intrinsically precarious.

While, then, every part of our country thus feels an immediate and particular interest in union, all the parts combined cannot fail to find in the united mass of means and efforts greater strength, greater resource, proportionably greater security from external danger, a less frequent interruption of their peace by foreign nations, and what is of inestimable value, they must derive from union an exemption from those broils and wars between themselves which so frequently afflict neighboring countries not tied together by the same governments, which their own rivalships alone would be sufficient to produce, but which opposite foreign alliances, attachments, and intrigues would stimulate and embitter. Hence, likewise, they will avoid the necessity of those overgrown military establishments which, under any form of government, are inauspicious to liberty, and which are to be regarded as particularly hostile to republican liberty. In this sense it is that your union ought to be considered as a main prop of your liberty, and that the love of the one ought to endear to you the preservation of the other....

Is there a doubt whether a common government can embrace so large a sphere? Let experience solve it. To listen to mere speculation in such a case were criminal. It is well worth a fair and full experiment. With such powerful and obvious motives to union affecting all parts of our country, while experience shall not have demonstrated its impracticability, there will always be reason to distrust the patriotism of those who in any quarter may endeavor to weaken its bands.

In contemplating the causes which may disturb our union it occurs as matter of serious concern that any ground should have been furnished for characterizing parties by geographical discriminations--Northern and Southern, Atlantic and Western -- whence designing men may endeavor to excite a belief that there is a real difference of local interests and views. One of the expedients of party to acquire influence within particular districts is to misrepresent the opinions and aims of other districts. You can not shield yourselves too much against the jealousies and heartburnings which spring from these misrepresentations; they tend to render alien to each other those who ought to be bound together by fraternal affection....

To the efficacy and permanency of your union a government for the whole is indispensable. No alliances, however strict, between the parts can be an adequate substitute. They must inevitably experience the infractions and interruptions which all alliances in all times have experienced. Sensible of this momentous truth, you have improved upon your first essay by the adoption of a Constitution of Government better calculated than your former for an intimate union and for the efficacious management of your common concerns. This Government, the offspring of our own choice, uninfluenced and unawed, adopted upon full investigation and mature deliberation, completely free in its principles, in the distribution of its powers, uniting security with energy, and containing within itself a provision for its own amendment, has a just claim to your confidence and your support. Respect for its authority, compliance with its laws, acquiescence in its measures, are duties enjoined by the fundamental maxims of true liberty. The basis of our political systems is the right of the people to make and to alter their constitutions of government. But the constitution which at any time exists till changed by an explicit and authentic act of the whole people is sacredly obligatory upon all. The very idea of the power and the right of the people to establish government presupposes the duty of every individual to obey the established government....

Toward the preservation of your Government and the permanency of your present happy state, it is requisite not only that you steadily discountenance irregular oppositions to its acknowledged authority, but also that you resist with care the spirit of innovation upon its principles, however specious the pretexts. One method of assault may be to effect in the forms of the Constitution alterations which will impair the energy of the system, and thus to undermine what can not be directly overthrown. In all the changes to which you may be invited remember that time and habit are at least as necessary to fix the true character of governments as of other human institutions; that experience is the surest standard by which to test the real tendency of the existing constitution of a country; that facility in changes upon the credit of mere hypothesis and opinion exposes to perpetual change, from the endless variety of hypothesis and opinion; and remember especially that for the efficient management of your common interests in a country so extensive as ours a government of as much vigor as is consistent with the perfect security of liberty is indispensable. Liberty itself will find in such a government, with powers properly distributed and adjusted, its surest guardian. It is, indeed, little else than a name where the government is too feeble to withstand the enterprises of faction, to con-fine each member of the society within the limits prescribed by the laws, and to maintain all in the secure and tranquil enjoyment of the rights of person and property.

I have already intimated to you the danger of parties in the State, with particular reference to the founding of them on geographical discriminations. Let me now take a more comprehensive view, and warn you in the most solemn manner against the baneful effects of the spirit of party generally.

This spirit, unfortunately, is inseparable from our nature, having its root in the strongest passions of the human mind. It exists under different shapes in all governments, more or less stifled, controlled, or repressed; but in those of the popular form it is seen in its greatest rankness and is truly their worst enemy....

It serves always to distract the public councils and enfeeble the public administration. It agitates the community with ill-founded jealousies and false alarms; kindles the animosity of one part against another; foments occasionally riot and insurrection. It opens the door to foreign influence and corruption, which finds a facilitated access to the government itself through the channels of party passion. Thus the policy and the will of one country are subjected to the policy and will of another.

There is an opinion that parties in free countries are useful checks upon the administration of the government, and serve to keep alive the spirit of liberty. This within certain limits is probably true; and in governments of a monarchical cast patriotism may look with indulgence, if not with favor, upon the spirit of party. But in those of the popular character, in governments purely elective, it is a spirit not to be encouraged. From their natural tendency it is certain there will always be enough of that spirit for every salutary purpose; and there being constant danger of excess, the effort ought to be by force of public opinion to mitigate and assuage it. A fire not to be quenched, it demands a uniform vigilance to prevent its bursting into a flame, lest, instead of warming, it should consume.

It is important, likewise, that the habits of thinking in a free country should inspire caution in those entrusted with its administration to confine themselves within their respective constitutional spheres, avoiding in the exercise of the powers of one department to encroach upon another. The spirit of encroachment tends to consolidate the powers of all the departments in one, and thus to create, whatever the form of government, a real despotism.... If in the opinion of the people the distribution or modification of the constitutional powers be in any particular wrong, let it be corrected by an amendment in the way which the Constitution designates. But let there be no change by usurpation; for though this in one instance may be the instrument of good, it is the customary weapon by which free governments are destroyed. The precedent must always greatly overbalance in permanent evil any partial or transient benefit which the use can at any time yield.

Of all the dispositions and habits which lead to political prosperity, religion and morality are indispensable supports. In vain would that man claim the tribute of patriotism who should labor to subvert these great pillars of human happiness -- these firmest props of the duties of men and citizens. The mere politician, equally with the pious man, ought to respect and to cherish them. A volume could not trace all their connections with private and public felicity. Let it simply be asked, Where is the security for property, for reputation, for life, if the sense of religious obligation desert the oaths which are the instruments of investigation in courts of justice? And let us with caution indulge the supposition that morality can be maintained without religion. Whatever may be conceded to the influence of refined education on minds of peculiar structure, reason and experience both forbid us to expect that national morality can prevail in exclusion of religious principle.

It is substantially true that virtue or morality is a necessary spring of popular government. The rule indeed extends with more or less force to every species of free government. Who that is a sincere friend to it can look with indifference upon attempts to shake the foundation of the fabric? Promote, then, as an object of primary importance, institutions for the general diffusion of knowledge. In proportion as the structure of a government gives force to public opinion, it is essential that public opinion should be enlightened.

As a very important source of strength and security, cherish public credit. One method of preserving it is to use it as sparingly as possible, avoiding occasions of expense by cultivating peace, but remembering also that timely disbursements to prepare for danger frequently prevent much greater disbursements to repel it; avoiding likewise the accumulation of debt, not only by shunning occasions of expense, but by vigorous exertions in time of peace to discharge the debts which unavoidable wars have occasioned, not ungenerously throwing upon posterity the burthen which we ourselves ought to bear....

Observe good faith and justice toward all nations. Cultivate peace and harmony with all. Religion and morality enjoin this conduct. And can it be that good policy does not equally enjoin it? It will be worthy of a free, enlightened, and at no distant period a great nation to give to mankind the magnanimous and too novel example of a people always guided by an exalted justice and benevolence. Who can doubt that in the course of time and things the fruits of such a plan would richly repay any temporary advantages which might be lost by a steady adherence to it? Can it be that Providence has not connected the permanent felicity of a nation with its virtue? The experiment, at least, is recommended by every sentiment which ennobles human nature. Alas! is it rendered impossible by its vices?

In the execution of such a plan nothing is more essential than that permanent, inveterate antipathies against particular nations and passionate attachments for others should be excluded, and that in place of them just and amicable feelings toward all should be cultivated. The nation which indulges toward another an habitual hatred or an habitual fondness is in some degree a slave. It is a slave to its animosity or to its affection, either of which is sufficient to lead it astray from its duty and its interest. Antipathy in one nation against another disposes each more readily to offer insult and injury, to lay hold of slight causes of umbrage, and to be haughty and intractable when accidental or trifling occasions of dispute occur.

So, likewise, a passionate attachment of one nation for another produces a variety of evils. Sympathy for the favorite nation, facilitating the illusion of an imaginary common interest in cases where no real common interest exists, and infusing into one the enmities of the other, betrays the former into a participation in the quarrels and wars of the latter without adequate inducement or justification. It leads also to concessions to the favorite nation of privileges denied to others, which is apt doubly to injure the nation making the concessions by unnecessarily parting with what ought to have been retained, and by exciting jealousy, ill will, and a disposition to retaliate in the parties from whom equal privileges are withheld; and it gives to ambitious, corrupted, or deluded citizens (who devote themselves to the favorite nation) facility to betray or sacrifice the interests of their own country without odium, sometimes even with popularity, gilding with the appearances of a virtuous sense of obligation, a commendable deference for public opinion, or a laudable zeal for public good the base or foolish compliances of ambition, corruption, or infatuation....

Against the insidious wiles of foreign influence (I conjure you to believe me, fellow-citizens) the jealousy of a free people ought to be constantly awake, since history and experience prove that foreign influence is one of the most baneful foes of republican government. But that jealousy, to be useful, must be impartial, else it becomes the instrument of the very influence to be avoided, instead of a defense against it. Excessive partiality for one foreign nation and excessive dislike of another cause those whom they actuate to see danger only on one side, and serve to veil and even second the arts of influence on the other. Real patriots who may resist the intrigues of the favorite are liable to become suspected and odious, while its tools and dupes usurp the applause and confidence of the people to surrender their interests.

The great rule of conduct for us in regard to foreign nations is, in extending our commercial relations to have with them as little political connection as possible. So far as we have already formed engagements let them be fulfilled with perfect good faith. Here let us stop.

Europe has a set of primary interests which to us have none or a very remote relation. Hence she must be engaged in frequent controversies, the causes of which are essentially foreign to our concerns. Hence, therefore, it must be unwise in us to implicate ourselves by artificial ties in the ordinary vicissitudes of her politics or the ordinary combinations and collisions of her friendships or enmities.

Our detached and distant situation invites and enables us to pursue a different course. If we remain one people, under an efficient government, the period is not far off when we may defy material injury from external annoyance; when we may take such an attitude as will cause the neutrality we may at any time resolve upon to be scrupulously respected; when belligerent nations, under the impossibility of making acquisitions upon us, will not lightly hazard the giving us provocation; when we may choose peace or war, as our interest, guided by justice, shall counsel.

Why forego the advantages of so peculiar a situation? Why quit our own to stand upon foreign ground? Why, by interweaving our destiny with that of any part of Europe, entangle our peace and prosperity in the toils of European ambition, rivalship, interest, humor, or caprice?

It is our true policy to steer clear of permanent alliances with any portion of the foreign world, so far, I mean, as we are now at liberty to do it, for let me not be understood as capable of patronizing infidelity to existing engagements. I hold the maxim no less applicable to public than to private affairs that honesty is always the best policy. I repeat, therefore, let those engagements be observed in their genuine sense. But in my opinion it is unnecessary and would be unwise to extend them.

Taking care always to keep ourselves by suitable establishments on a respectable defensive posture, we may safely trust to temporary alliances for extraordinary emergencies.

Harmony, liberal intercourse with all nations are recommended by policy, humanity, and interest. But even our commercial policy should hold an equal and impartial hand, neither seeking nor granting exclusive favors or preferences; consulting the natural course of things; diffusing and diversifying by gentle means the streams of commerce, but forcing nothing; establishing with powers so disposed, in order to give trade a stable course, to define the rights of our merchants, and to enable the Government to support them, conventional rules of intercourse, the best that present circumstances and mutual opinion will permit, but temporary and liable to be from time to time abandoned or varied as experience and circumstances shall dictate; constantly keeping in view that it is folly in one nation to look for disinterested favors from another; that it must pay with a portion of its independence for whatever it may accept under that character; that by such acceptance it may place itself in the condition of having given equivalents for nominal favors, and yet of being reproached with ingratitude for not giving more. There can be no greater error than to expect or calculate upon real favors from nation to nation. It is an illusion which experience must cure, which a just pride ought to discard....

Though in reviewing the incidents of my Administration I am unconscious of intentional error, I am nevertheless too sensible of my defects not to think it probable that I may have committed many errors. Whatever they may be, I fervently beseech the Almighty to avert or mitigate the evils to which they may tend. I shall also carry with me the hope that my country will never cease to view them with indulgence, and that, after forty-five years of my life dedicated to its service with an upright zeal, the faults of incompetent abilities will be consigned to oblivion, as myself must soon be to the mansions of rest.

Relying on its kindness in this as in other things, and actuated by that fervent love toward it which is so natural to a man who views in it the native soil of himself and his progenitors for several generations, I anticipate with pleasing expectation that retreat in which I promise myself to realize without alloy the sweet enjoyment of partaking in the midst of my fellow-citizens the benign influence of good laws under a free government -- the ever-favorite object of my heart, and the happy reward, as I trust, of our mutual cares, labors, and dangers.

Monroe Doctrine

The Monroe Doctrine was about foreign policy. It included the following policies:

- European countries had to respect the boundaries of the New World
- Old World powers such as England and France could keep their existing colonies but could not found any new ones
- America would institute democracy across the continent

The Monroe Doctrine curbed fear of the American's expanding into the West Indies.

The Exponential Growth of the United States, Socially, Economically and Culturally

THE SOCIAL CANVAS

The United States is the fourth largest country in the world, owning about 3,615,123 square miles. There are fifty States in addition to the District of Columbia, spanning over 3000 miles from the Atlantic to the Pacific. From Canada in the North to the Gulf of Mexico in the South, it covers a distance of 1,598 miles. It has everything from the coastal plains to the Appalachian Highlands to the central lowland to the Great Plains to the Rocky Mountains to the intermountain Plateaus and to the Pacific Mountain System. It is endowed with a bounty of natural resources. Climate differs from place to place depending upon the latitude. The Constitution of the United States guarantees religious freedom for all its subjects. At the birth of the nation in the year 1776, a little over 90% of the people were farmers. The War of 1812 saw goods from England to the United States drying up. It had become imperative for Americans to build their own factories and make inventions and innovations in manufacturing, management and technology. There were many, many woolen and cotton mills by 1815. The peace between England and America slowed down the growth. But after the Civil War a veritable revolution - the Industrial Revolution - took America by storm. The telegraph, electric bulb, railroads, printing machinery, typewriter, telephone exchange, mechanized agricultural equipment and so on were all invented.

The social fabric of the United States gradually marched towards industrialization and hence there was a veritable population shift from rural to urban cities. Though the Indians were there in America well before anyone else landed, the civilization that enveloped the Americans was not that of Indians but that of Europeans.

THE IMMIGRANTS

The people who came to America before the American Revolution were known as Colonists. Those who landed after the Revolution were known as Immigrants. Over 37 million immigrants landed in the United States between 1830 and 1930. Most of them came from Western Europe - England, Ireland, France, Germany, and the Scandinavian countries. After 1890, the immigrants were mainly from Eastern and southern Europe - Poland, Russia, Greece, Italy, Hungary and Austria. The immigrants did face resistance. In 1798, the Alien and Sedition Act was mainly aimed at Irish and French immigrants. In 1850 the "Know Nothing" Party was formed to resist immigration of German and Irish people. In 1920's the Ku Klux Klan denounced all foreign immigrants in the United States. But sane counsel prevailed with the majority. Without the immigrants, the U.S. would never move forward in almost every sphere of life in a breath-taking span of time.

The United States of America has a rich heritage. The heritage to see the nation as a conglomeration of immigrants. The great seal of the United States of America depicts; of course, in Latin: "…E PLURIBUS UNUM…." Which translated in English means "…OUT OF MANY, ONE…" The United States of America was created out of the people of the whole world.

THE LOUISIANA PURCHASE

In 1803 Thomas Jefferson purchased a large area of land from the France. He was able to double the size of the country for only 15 million dollars. Jefferson knew that as President he was not authorized to purchase land, but he seized the incredible opportunity when it arose. France sold the land because Napoleon needed the money to fund his campaign to conquer most of Europe.

Because American ships were constantly seized by the England and France, who were looking for supplies to help their side in the war, Jefferson passed the Embargo Act in 1807 which prohibited trading with Europe. The Embargo Act hurt America much more that England or France. It caused an economic depression until it was repealed in 1809.

Jefferson wanted to map the Louisiana Territory so he approved Lewis and Clark to lead the "Corps of Discovery" expedition.

THE ECONOMIC FABRIC

From 1776 when ninety percent of the people of the country depended mainly on agriculture, to the present day, where the United States is rated to be the Super Economic Power, the march has been arduous; single minded devotion, hard work and a spirit of innovation got them exceptional advancement in the areas of industry, commerce, and, trade.

In 1793, Eli Whitney invented the cotton gin. This revolutionized the cotton industry.

In 1700 prisoners were brought as workers. Tobacco plantations were established in the South. Large paddy and sugar plantations were also established in the South.

In 1704 the Boston News Letter, the world's first newspaper was launched in Boston.

In 1844 Samuel Morse's telegraphic codes were firmly established between America and England.

Between 1861 and 1865, railroads were built connecting all parts of the United States. Industries and business developed in cities.

In 1868 the typewriter was invented.

In 1876 Alex and Graham Bell's telephone was patented. In 1878, the first telephone exchange was built in New Haven.

In 1882 the first electric bulb was invented. All those inventions brought excellent returns to the United States. Industry and Commerce leaped to new levels. Imports and Exports scaled new heights. Today the United States is the world's leading industrialized nation. Approximately 60% of the manufacturing activity lies in the States east of the Mississippi River and north of the Ohio River.

In the agricultural front, there are approximately 3-million farms with an average size of about 450 acres. In 1820, an agricultural worker produced enough food for himself and three others. Today an agricultural worker, on average, is able to supply food for himself and about sixty others. From corn, to wheat, to cotton, to fruits - they produce everything. The Northeast is full of dairy farmland.

The United States produces about 28 to 32% of the world's electricity production.

EDUCATION

Free public schools are instituted by law and are aided and nurtured by taxation. More than twenty percent of the population was illiterate a hundred years ago, but today less than one percent are unable to read. Education is compulsory for both boys and girls. Excellent opportunities for higher education are present.

ARTS & MUSIC

There are thousands of symphony orchestras. In public schools, thousands of students receive training each year in singing or instrumental music. There are thousands of professional painters, sculptors and other artists. Originally, in the early colonial times and immediately thereafter, the architecture reflected colonial British style. In the early 19th century, the imperial style was the American version of classical architecture. Gradually the style changed with urbanization and condominiums and skyscrapers became the order of the day.

SCULPTURE

Native Indians were known to be great sculptors. Wood carving was their main profession. What lacked in sophistication was made up by excellent rustic charm. Augustus Saint-Ganders (1848-1901) and Daniel Chester French (1850-1931) brought American sculpture into international fame. The equestrian statue of St. Gauden's monument to General Sherman is a piece of exquisite sculpting. The statue of Abraham Lincoln in the Lincoln memorial in Washington, one of Daniel Chester French's magnum opus, depicts a nineteen-foot seated but brooding figure of the president and it is considered unique.

Gaston Lachaise (1882-1935) is associated with Modern Sculpture. Sculptures representing abstract themes are known to be associated with names like: Louis Nevelson, Seymour Lipton, Joseph Cornel, Theodore Roszak, and Leonard Baskin.

LITERATURE

American literature started flowering after the end of the Revolutionary War in 1783. Washington Irving wrote "Rip Van Winkle "and "The Legend of Sleepy Hollow." Writers like Fennimore Cooper, William Cullen Bryant (1794-1878), Edgar Allen Poe (1809-49), Ralph Waldo Emerson (1803-82), Henry David Thoreau (1817-62), Nathaniel Hawthorne (1804-64) were some of the writers who lend potency to American Literature. Herman Melville's (1819-91) "Moby Dick" is considered to be one of the greatest American sea tales ever told There were many, many more writers of repute who embellished the American Literate like Mark Twain, and P.G. Wodehouse. Harriet Beech Stowe wrote "Uncle Tom's Cabin."

Sample Test Questions

1) Who wrote "Leaves of Grass"?

   A) Francis Scott Key
   B) Dred Scott
   C) Harriet Beecher Stowe
   D) Henry James
   E) Walt Whitman

The correct answer is E:) Walt Whitman.

2) What was the name of the first English settlement to survive colonization?

   A) Roanoke
   B) Jamestown
   C) Charleston
   D) Plymouth
   E) Raleigh

The correct answer is B:) Jamestown. Roanoke and Raleigh were both earlier than Jamestown, but both failed.

3) The gold rush of 1849 sent settlers to what state?

   A) Utah
   B) California
   C) Florida
   D) Nevada
   E) Oregon

The correct answer is B:) California.

4) In what way were slaves and indentured servants similar?

   A) Both were allowed to seek an education.
   B) Both had to provide food and shelter for themselves.
   C) Both could be bought and sold.
   D) Neither could ever have the opportunity to vote.
   E) Both A and C

The correct answer is C:) Both could be bought and sold. D is incorrect because indentured servants could vote once they had been freed, B is incorrect because owners did provide clothing and shelter (though it was generally inadequate), and A is incorrect because neither could educate themselves.

5) Which Amendment awards power to individual states?

   A) 1st Amendment
   B) 2nd Amendment
   C) 5th Amendment
   D) 6th Amendment
   E) 10th Amendment

The correct answer is E:) 10th Amendment.

6) Which of the following MOST correctly lists the most populous colonial cities?

   A) Charleston, Albany, Portsmouth
   B) Boston, Raleigh, Salem
   C) New York, Philadelphia, Boston
   D) Philadelphia, Charleston, Salem
   E) Boston, Albany, Atlanta

The correct answer is C:) New York, Philadelphia, Boston. Charleston was the only city that rivaled these three.

7) When the French demanded tribute from America before speaking with ambassadors it was called

   A) French-American War
   B) Louisiana Purchase
   C) Intercourse Act
   D) XYZ Affair
   E) None of the above

The correct answer is D:) XYZ Affair.

8) Which of the following was NOT a slave rebellion?

   A) The Stono Rebellion
   B) Shay's Rebellion
   C) Prosser's Rebellion
   D) Harper's Ferry
   E) None of the above

The correct answer is B:) Shay's Rebellion. This rebellion involved farmers upset about not being paid for their involvement in the Revolutionary War.

9) Lincoln was assassinated by?

   A) Henry Locke
   B) John Wilkes Booth
   C) John Williams
   D) Henry Longfellow
   E) None of the above

The correct answer is B:) John Wilkes Booth.

10) Which of the following was dictated by the 14th Amendment?

   A) Equal protection under the law for blacks and whites.
   B) All persons born in the United States, or naturalized, are citizens.
   C) Due process for all citizens, no matter what race.
   D) The federal government will not pay any debt for the loss or emancipation of any slave.
   E) All of the above

The correct answer is E:) All of the above. The 14th Amendment was passed after the Civil War.

11) What percentage of the Army during the Civil War was African American?

   A) 5%
   B) 10%
   C) 20%
   D) 25%
   E) 40%

The correct answer is B:) 10%.

12) Eliza Lucas Pickney is famed for being the person who introduced which product and made it a successful crop?

   A) Tobacco
   B) Cotton
   C) Indigo
   D) Rice
   E) Corn

The correct answer is C:) Indigo. At one time, it was argued that indigo was even more profitable than cotton.

13) While men were away at war, women did what?

   A) Ran farms
   B) Worked as nurses
   C) Did manual labor
   D) Worked as spies
   E) All of the above

The correct answer is E:) All of the above.

14) The Powhatan Confederacy was

   I. A collection of Native American tribes which was especially prominent in the Virginia area in the 17th century.
   II. Originally composed of the Powhatan, Arrohateck, Appamattuck, Pamunkey, Mattaponi, and the Chiskiack tribes.
   III. Founded by the natives in 1607 to agree upon a way to handle relations with the new English settlers of Jamestown.

   A) I only
   B) I and II only
   C) II and III only
   D) I and III only
   E) I, II and III

The correct answer is B:) I and II only. The six tribes listed in II were the original members of the Powhattan Confederacy; however, over time its reach extended to include more than 30 tribes. The Confederacy was established before the English settlers arrived.

15) The person who assassinated Lincoln shouted the following after committing the murder "Sic simper tyrannis." What does it mean?

   A) No more tyrants
   B) The end to tyrants
   C) Death to tyrants
   D) Thus always to tyrants
   E) To our tyrant

The correct answer is D:) Thus always to tyrants.

16) In 1680, the Pueblo Indians fought for independence from which nation?

   A) Spain
   B) France
   C) Portugal
   D) England
   E) Belgium

The correct answer is A:) Spain.

17) The Morill Tariff Act did what?

   A) Increased tariffs on imported goods
   B) Decreased tariffs on goods from the South
   C) Created a national currency
   D) Lifted the tariff on sugar
   E) None of the above

The correct answer is A:) Increased tariffs on imported goods.

18) Alexis de Tocqueville wrote a study on the political and social structure of the United States called

   A) A Criticism of America
   B) Democracy is America
   C) The Old Regime and the Revolution
   D) A Study on American Civilization
   E) The Complete Works of Alexis de Tocqueville: A study of the Americas

The correct answer is B:) Democracy in America. It was published in the late 1830s.

19) Dred Scott was

   A) A lawyer
   B) A politician
   C) A slave
   D) A judge
   E) A landowner

The correct answer is C:) A slave.

20) Which Amendment guarantees the right against self-incrimination?

   A) First
   B) Third
   C) Fifth
   D) Eighth
   E) Tenth

The correct answer is C:) Fifth.

21) Who was a key conductor in the Underground Railroad?

   A) Rosa Parks
   B) Harriet Tubman
   C) Francis Scott Key
   D) Dred Scott
   E) Henry Mills

The correct answer is B:) Harriet Tubman.

22) In 1838-1839, Cherokee Indians faced hunger, disease and death due to which event?

   A) Smallpox
   B) King Philip's War
   C) Trail of Tears
   D) The Seminole War
   E) The Sand Creek Massacre

The correct answer is C:) Trail of Tears. Over a quarter of the Cherokee Nation died during the forced migration from Mississippi to Oklahoma.

23) Who wrote "Uncle Tom's Cabin"?

   A) Francis Scott Key
   B) Dred Scott
   C) Harriet Beecher Stowe
   D) Henry James
   E) Walt Whitman

The correct answer is C:) Harriet Beecher Stowe.

24) Which of the following was NOT an advantage held by the British in the Revolutionary War?

   A) A more advanced and trained military
   B) Greater supplies and resources
   C) A developed and powerful navy
   D) A greater stake in the outcome of the war
   E) All of the above are British advantages

The correct answer is D:) A greater stake in the outcome of the war. The colonists were fighting for their beliefs and way of life, whereas the members of the British military were just fighting because it was their job.

25) Who wrote "The Star Spangled Banner"?

    A) Francis Scott Key
    B) Dred Scott
    C) Harriet Beecher Stowe
    D) Henry James
    E) Walt Whitman

The correct answer is A:) Francis Scott Key.

26) Which of the following is a correct statement about the economic system used colonial times?

    A) It was later traded for the more successful mercantile system.
    B) It favored an excess of imports above exports.
    C) It relied on the standard of living as a measure of a country's prosperity.
    D) It involved a limited amount of government control over trade.
    E) It was based on the idea that there was a limited amount of wealth in the world.

The correct answer is E:) It was based on the idea that there was a limited amount of wealth in the world. This meant that one country could only get rich at the expense of another. This created high government involvement in trade and an emphasis on the generation of wealth. It was called the mercantile system and was later traded for the laissez fair system.

27) Who gave the sermon "City Upon a Hill"?

    A) John Winthrop
    B) Thomas Paine
    C) John Dickenson
    D) Jonathan Edwards
    E) George Whitefield

The correct answer is A:) John Winthrop.

28) What was the first legislative body in the Americas?

   A) House of Burgesses
   B) Senate
   C) First Continental Congress
   D) House of Representatives
   E) None of the above

The correct answer is A:) House of Burgesses. This was set up in Virginia in 1619.

29) Who wrote "Common Sense"?

   A) John Winthrop
   B) Thomas Paine
   C) John Dickenson
   D) Jonathan Edwards
   E) George Whitefield

The correct answer is B:) Thomas Paine.

30) Which group drafted and signed the Declaration of Independence?

   A) First Continental Congress
   B) Son's of Liberty
   C) Continental Association
   D) Second Continental Congress
   E) None of the above

The correct answer is D:) Second Continental Congress.

31) Who wrote "Letters from a Farmer in Pennsylvania"?

   A) John Winthrop
   B) Thomas Paine
   C) John Dickenson
   D) Jonathan Edwards
   E) George Whitefield

The correct answer is C:) John Dickenson.

32) Which English colony became a haven for those seeking religious freedom and tolerance?

   A) Massachusetts
   B) Virginia
   C) Rhode Island
   D) South Carolina
   E) Maryland

The correct answer is C:) Rhode Island. Jews and Quakers both sought refuge in Rhode Island which was founded by Roger Williams and Anne Hutchinson.

33) Which preacher did skits and dramatizations in his sermons?

   A) John Winthrop
   B) Thomas Paine
   C) John Dickenson
   D) Jonathan Edwards
   E) George Whitefield

The correct answer is E:) George Whitefield.

34) By the mid nineteenth century, which book was the standard reading textbook for schools?

   A) The Bible
   B) Webster's Dictionary
   C) The Scarlet Letter
   D) McGuffey Reader
   E) The Farmers Almanac

The correct answer is D:) McGuffey Reader. This book was first published in 1836 and was written by William McGuffey.

35) Renaissance means

   A) Anew
   B) To give life
   C) Rebirth
   D) Changing of times
   E) None of the above

The correct answer is C:) Rebirth.

36) What officially ended the practice of slavery in the United States?

   A) The 13th Amendment
   B) The Emancipation Proclamation
   C) The Gettysburg Address
   D) The 14th Amendment
   E) The 20th Amendment

The correct answer is A:) The 13th Amendment. The Emancipation Proclamation freed all slaves in "areas of rebellion," but the 13th Amendment officially ended the practice from a legal standpoint.

37) Which Amendment guarantees the right to a speedy trial?

   A) 1st Amendment
   B) 2nd Amendment
   C) 5th Amendment
   D) 6th Amendment
   E) 10th Amendment

The correct answer is D:) 6th Amendment.

38) Who is considered to be the first black woman to make a living from her writing?

   A) Ida B. Wells
   B) Harriet Beecher Stowe
   C) Sojourner Truth
   D) Phillis Wheatly
   E) None of the above

The correct answer is D:) Phillis Wheatly. As a young slave, she was given the rare opportunity to learn to read and write and was considered a prodigy.

39) Which of the following where Columbus' ships?

   A) Nina
   B) Pinta
   C) Santa Maria
   D) Answers A, B, C
   E) Mayflower

The correct answer is D:) Answers A, B, C.

40) Who gave the famous speech "Ain't I a Woman?" and was a traveling preacher who advocated the rights of women and slaves?

   A) Harriet Beecher Stowe
   B) Phillis Wheatly
   C) Sojourner Truth
   D) Ida B Wells
   E) Frederick Douglass

The correct answer is C:) Sojourner Truth.

41) Who was first to discover the new world?

   A) Portugal
   B) Columbus
   C) France
   D) Vikings
   E) Dutch

The correct answer is D:) Vikings.

42) Emma Willard was an advocate of

   A) Freedom of speech
   B) Abolition of slavery
   C) Temperance
   D) Education for women
   E) None of the above

The correct answer is D:) Education for women. She worked her whole life for the education of women. During her life she both taught female students and instructed teachers on how to better teach female students.

43) Columbus sailed under the patronage of what country?

   A) Portugal
   B) France
   C) Italy
   D) Spain
   E) Holland

The correct answer is D:) Spain.

44) Brook Farm, Oneida and New Harmony were all

   A) Early colonial settlements
   B) Attempts at utopian society
   C) Sites of major Civil War battles
   D) Large southern plantations
   E) None of the above

The correct answer is B:) Attempts at utopian society. New Harmony was established by Robert Owen and lasted only two years. Oneida was formed based on the idea of group marriages to create equality among members.

45) The men who attended the Constitutional Convention to create a government were known as:

   A) Founding fathers
   B) Framers
   C) Signers
   D) Congress
   E) None of the above

The correct answer is B:) Framers.

46) Who is reported to have told Harriet Beecher Stowe "so you are the little woman who wrote the book that started this great war"?

   A) Francis Scott Key
   B) John Jay
   C) Abraham Lincoln
   D) Henry James
   E) Walt Whitman

The correct answer is C:) Abraham Lincoln. The President reportedly told this to Harriet Beecher Stowe when they first met after she had written "Uncle Tom's Cabin."

47) The Three-fifths Compromise refers to what?

   A) The amount of states in the union
   B) The number of votes to a state
   C) The population of a state
   D) The accounting relating to slaves versus free people
   E) The veto power

The correct answer is D:) The accounting relating to slaves versus free people.

48) Which of the following does NOT correctly match a country with its export in the Triangular Trade system?

   A) Africa; Slaves
   B) West Indies; Sugar
   C) England; Manufactured goods
   D) American Colonies; Fish, Grain, and Lumber
   E) All of the above are correct

The correct answer is E:) All of the above are correct. Each stage of trade relied on the goods which the countries produced. England had luxury manufactured goods like glass and tea, the colonies had raw materials, Africa had slaves and the West Indies produced sugar and molasses.

49) Who wrote "The Federalist Papers"?

   A) Francis Scott Key
   B) Alexander Hamilton
   C) Harriet Beecher Stowe
   D) Henry James
   E) Walt Whitman

The correct answer is B:) Alexander Hamilton.

50) Which president was responsible for the Louisiana Purchase?

   A) George Washington
   B) Thomas Jefferson
   C) John Adams
   D) James Madison
   E) Zachary Taylor

The correct answer is B:) Thomas Jefferson. Though he wasn't sure it was within his constitutional rights, he couldn't pass up the opportunity to double the country's size with one land purchase.

51) The idea that one branch of government is supervised by another is called

   A) Checks and balances
   B) Legislative
   C) Democracy
   D) House and Senate
   E) Congress

The correct answer is A:) Checks and balances.

52) Who was the first person to run for President as a republican candidate?

   A) Martin Van Buren
   B) Abraham Lincoln
   C) George Washington
   D) John C Fremont
   E) Aaron Burr

The correct answer is D:) John C Fremont. However, Abraham Lincoln was the first Republican candidate to be elected.

53) Which Amendment protects freedom of religion, speech, press, etc.?

   A) 1st Amendment
   B) 2nd Amendment
   C) 5th Amendment
   D) 6th Amendment
   E) 10th Amendment

The correct answer is A:) 1st Amendment.

When colonists began encroaching on Indian lands, the Indians decided to attack. Around half of the currently existing English settlements were attacked throughout the course of the conflict. Eventually the tides turned in the colonists favor, and a treaty was signed at Casco Bay.

54) The above statement describes which war?

    A) King Philip's War
    B) The French and Indian War
    C) Little Big Horn
    D) The Seven Years War
    E) None of the above

The correct answer is A:) King Philip's War.

55) Horace Mann fought for

    A) Prison reform
    B) Prostitution reform
    C) Education reform
    D) Insane-asylum reform
    E) Medial reform

The correct answer is C:) Education reform.

56) John James Audubon was most famous for

    A) His participation in the Great Awakening.
    B) His economic theories during the Enlightenment.
    C) His collection of paintings of birds.
    D) Writing the pamphlet Common Sense.
    E) Being the first Republican presidential candidate.

The correct answer is C:) His collection of paintings of birds.

57) John Greenleaf Whittier was known as

   A) A romantic
   B) A dark romantic
   C) A transcendentalist
   D) A creator of lithographs
   E) None of the above

The correct answer is A:) A romantic.

58) What is significant about Oberlin College in Ohio?

   A) It was the first college to admit former slaves.
   B) It was the first college established after the Revolutionary War.
   C) It was the first college to have an integrated faculty.
   D) It was the first coeducational college.
   E) None of the above

The correct answer is D:) It was the first coeducational college.

59) Which Amendment is about the right to bear arms?

   A) 1st Amendment
   B) 2nd Amendment
   C) 5th Amendment
   D) 6th Amendment
   E) 10th Amendment

The correct answer is B:) 2nd Amendment.

60) Why did President Pierce send Commodore Perry to Japan?

   A) In an attempt to open up trade
   B) To intimidate them from joining WWII
   C) To protect them from attack by the Chinese
   D) To destroy the capital city
   E) None of the above

The correct answer is A:) In an attempt to open up trade. While the move did help pull Japan out of isolation, they did not yet agree to sign any formal declarations.

61) Which Amendment guarantees due process?

   A) 1st Amendment
   B) 2nd Amendment
   C) 5th Amendment
   D) 6th Amendment
   E) 10th Amendment

The correct answer is C:) 5th Amendment.

62) Why did the Mormon pioneers settle in Utah?

   I. They were fleeing persecution in other states and Utah was both isolated and remote.
   II. Their prophet declared that it was the place he had seen in a vision.
   III. Their original destination had been California, but due to the weather they couldn't continue.

   A) I only
   B) II only
   C) III only
   D) I and II only
   E) I and III only

The correct answer is D:) I and II. The Mormon pioneers never intended to go to California.

63) Dorothea Dix reformed

   A) Prostitution
   B) Prisons
   C) Insane-asylums
   D) Both A and B
   E) Both B and C

The correct answer is E:) Both B and C.

64) Which of the following was NOT an advantage held by the Union during the Civil War?

    A) Better trained military leaders
    B) More industrialized economy
    C) More railways and supply lines
    D) Both A and C
    E) None of the above

The correct answer is A:) Better trained military leaders. Most of the country's best military leaders were in the South. Also, all but one of the country's military schools were in the south.

65) Edgar Allan Poe was known as

    A) A romantic
    B) A dark romantic
    C) A transcendentalist
    D) A creator of lithographs
    E) None of the above

The correct answer is B:) A dark romantic.

66) Which of the following battles consisted of a victory for the colonists that convinced the French to aid their cause in the Revolutionary War?

    A) Yorktown
    B) Princeton
    C) Bunker Hill
    D) Saratoga
    E) Trenton

The correct answer is D:) Saratoga. The French had been hesitating to enter the war, but after seeing the British surrender six generals, 300 officers and 5,500 soldiers they were finally convinced.

67) Louisa May Alcott was known as

   A) A romantic
   B) A dark romantic
   C) A transcendentalist
   D) A creator of lithographs
   E) None of the above

The correct answer is A:) A romantic.

68) Why did President Lincoln wait as long as he did to issue the Emancipation Proclamation?

   A) He did not initially disagree with slavery and it took that long for Congress to convince him.
   B) He did not believe it constitutional unless the war had continued for a certain amount of time.
   C) He waited until the Union was clearly losing and issued it so that the free slaves could fight.
   D) It took that long for it to be written and approved by Congress.
   E) He waited until they Union started winning major victories and he believed it would have the support of the people.

The correct answer is E:) He waited until they Union started winning major victories and he believed it would have the support of the people.

69) Ralph Waldo Emerson was known as

   A) A romantic
   B) A dark romantic
   C) A transcendentalist
   D) A creator of lithographs
   E) None of the above

The correct answer is C:) A transcendentalist.

70) The Hudson River School was

   A) The first southern school to practice integration.
   B) The first functioning art school in the United States.
   C) The first public school in the United States.
   D) The first college open to individuals who were once slaves.
   E) None of the above

The correct answer is B:) The first functioning art school in the United States.

71) Henry David Thoreau was known as

   A) A romantic
   B) A dark romantic
   C) A transcendentalist
   D) A creator of lithographs
   E) None of the above

The correct answer is C:) A transcendentalist.

72) After the Glorious Revolution dethroned James II in England, the colonial members of New York rebelled against James' agent Lieut. Gov. Francis Nicholson and began running the colony themselves. This even is referred to as

   A) Shay's Rebellion
   B) Dorr Rebellion
   C) Fries's Rebellion
   D) Bacon's Rebellion
   E) Leisler's Rebellion

The correct answer is E:) Leisler's Rebellion.

73) Herman Melville was known as

   A) A romantic
   B) A dark romantic
   C) A transcendentalist
   D) A creator of lithographs
   E) None of the above

The correct answer is B:) A dark romantic.

74) The founding fathers first attempt at creating a government yielded the

   A) United States Constitution
   B) Declaration of Independence
   C) Articles of Confederation
   D) Declaration of Rights
   E) Magna Carta

The correct answer is C:) Articles of Confederation. This documents created a weak national government and because of this weren't able to function effectively.

75) Currier and Ives were known as

   A) A romantic
   B) A dark romantic
   C) A transcendentalist
   D) A creator of lithographs
   E) None of the above

The correct answer is D:) A creator of lithographs.

76) "The said States hereby severally enter into a firm league of friendship with each other, for their common defense, the security of their liberties, and their mutual and general welfare, binding themselves to assist each other..." This quote is from which document?

   A) United States Constitution
   B) Declaration of Independence
   C) Articles of Confederation
   D) Emancipation Proclamation
   E) Bill of Rights

The correct answer is C:) Articles of Confederation. The Articles created a weak national government, as is shown by the fact that the States are referred to as a "league of friendship" and not a collective union.

77) Nathaniel Hawthorne was known as

   A) A romantic
   B) A dark romantic
   C) A transcendentalist
   D) A creator of lithographs
   E) None of the above

The correct answer is B:) A dark romantic.

78) Which of the following people was responsible for founding Pennsylvania?

   A) Roger Williams
   B) Anne Hutchinson
   C) Thomas Hooker
   D) Peter Zenger
   E) William Penn

The correct answer is E:) William Penn. The King had owed Penn's father a large sum of money, so when his father died Penn asked for an allotment of land as a payment of the debt. The King named the area Penn's Woods, or, Pennsylvania.

79) Henry Wadsworth Longfellow was known as

   A) A romantic
   B) A dark romantic
   C) A transcendentalist
   D) A creator of lithographs
   E) None of the above

The correct answer is A:) A romantic.

80) Who founded Providence, Rhode Island?

   A) Roger Williams
   B) Thomas Hooker
   C) James White
   D) Sir Walter Raleigh
   E) Anne Hutchinson

The correct answer is A:) Roger Williams. After upsetting the Puritans by preaching in their churches, the King of England granted Roger Williams a charter.

81) Walt Whitman was known as

　　A) A romantic
　　B) A dark romantic
　　C) A transcendentalist
　　D) A creator of lithographs
　　E) None of the above

The correct answer is C:) A transcendentalist.

82) What treaty fully ended the Mexican War?

　　A) Treaty of Washington
　　B) Treaty of Cahuenga
　　C) Treaty of Guadalupe Hidalgo
　　D) Mallarino Bidlack Treaty
　　E) Adams-Onis Treaty

The correct answer is C:) Treaty of Guadalupe Hidalgo. The treaty was signed in 1848. The Treaty of Cahuenga ended the war in California, but the Treaty of Guadalupe Hidalgo fully ended the war.

83) Who invented the cotton gin?

　　A) Eli Whitney
　　B) John Dickenson
　　C) Alexander Bell
　　D) Henry James
　　E) None of the above

The correct answer is A:) Eli Whitney.

84) The trial of Peter Zenger in 1737 was most associated with which of the following issues?

　　A) Freedom of speech
　　B) Freedom of religion
　　C) Cruel and unusual punishment
　　D) Freedom of the press
　　E) Freedom to bear arms

The correct answer is D:) Freedom of the press. He was a newspaper editor for a paper which printed harsh criticisms about New York Governor Cosby. He was sued for printing libelous information, but won on the defense that if it was true it wasn't libel. This was a major step for freedom of the press.

85) Who wrote "Ten Nights in a Bar-Room and What I Saw There"?

   A) Nathaniel Hawthorne
   B) T.S. Arthur
   C) Herman Melville
   D) John Deere
   E) Henry David Thoreau

The correct answer is B:) T.S. Arthur.

86) Which of the following people was responsible for founding Hartford, Connecticut?

   A) Roger Williams
   B) Anne Hutchinson
   C) Thomas Hooker
   D) Peter Zenger
   E) William Penn

The correct answer is C:) Thomas Hooker. He led a group of people from the Massachusetts Bay colony in 1636 and they received a charter from the King of England in 1662.

87) Who wrote "Walden"?

   A) Nathaniel Hawthorne
   B) T.S. Arthur
   C) Herman Melville
   D) John Deere
   E) Henry David Thoreau

The correct answer is E:) Henry David Thoreau.

88) What would most likely be found at the center of a city in a northern colony?

   A) A large plantation
   B) A church
   C) A tax collection center
   D) A store
   E) A city building

The correct answer is B:) A church. The northern colonies were literally centered around churches, with many of the colonies being founded by religious groups.

89) The temperance movement regulated what?

   A) Prisons
   B) Prostitution
   C) Alcohol
   D) Slaves
   E) None of the above

The correct answer is C:) Alcohol.

90) What was the ruling in the Dred Scott case?

   A) Scott should be freed because he was in a free state.
   B) Scott had no right to sue because he was property and not a citizen.
   C) If Scott had sued earlier then he could have been freed, but because he waited so long the court was not going to hear the full trial.
   D) That not only should Scott be freed, the entire state of Mississippi should no longer be allowed to practice slavery.
   E) None of the above

The correct answer is B:) Scott had no right to sue because he was property and not a citizen. Dred Scott was a slave who sued for his freedom when his owner moved to a free state, but the Supreme Court ruled against him.

91) She called for social and political equality for women

   A) Dorothea Dix
   B) Elizabeth Cady Stanton
   C) Harriett Beecher Stowe
   D) Louisa Alcott
   E) Emily Dickenson

The correct answer is B:) Elizabeth Cady Stanton.

92) "We hold these truths to be self-evident, that all men are created equal, that they are endowed by their Creator with certain unalienable rights, that among these are life, liberty and the pursuit of happiness." This quote is from which document?

   A) United States Constitution
   B) Declaration of Independence
   C) Articles of Confederation
   D) Emancipation Proclamation
   E) Bill of Rights

The correct answer is B:) Declaration of Independence.

93) Of the following, this is the greatest discovery in manufacturing

   A) Steel plow
   B) Cotton gin
   C) Interchangeable parts
   D) Mower-reaper
   E) Moveable type

The correct answer is C:) Interchangeable parts.

94) Which of the following statements is TRUE of the First Great Awakening?

   A) Individuals began to see less of a personal role in religion and worship.
   B) The Great Awakening supported a decrease in the religious involvement of the laity.
   C) It consisted only of one preacher, George Whitefield, spurring members of his own congregation to be more vigilant in their worship.
   D) Along with heightening church attendance, it stimulated an interest in reading and the creation of schools. The movement favored a personal approach to religion.
   E) None of the above

The correct answer is D:) Along with heightening church attendance, it stimulated an interest in reading and the creation of schools. The movement favored a personal approach to religion.

95) Which President had a largely abolitionist cause?

   A) Thomas Jefferson
   B) Benjamin Franklin
   C) Abraham Lincoln
   D) John Adams
   E) Alexander Hamilton

The correct answer is C:) Abraham Lincoln.

96) Which of the following cases involved state's rights and the sanctity of contracts?

   A) Charles River Bridge v. Warren Bridge
   B) Dartmouth College v. Woodward
   C) Gibbons v. Ogden
   D) Fletcher v. Peck
   E) Prigg v. Pennsylvania

The correct answer is A:) Charles River Bridge v. Warren Bridge. The implications of the case were that the state of Massachusetts did have the right to issue a charter, and it wasn't a violation of the Charles River Bridge company's charter. It was seen as boost to state's rights.

97) Who was nicknamed "Unconditional Surrender"?

   A) Ulysses S. Grant
   B) Stephen Douglas
   C) George Washington
   D) Robert E. Lee
   E) None of the above

The correct answer is A:) Ulysses S. Grant.

98) Which was the first state to secede from the Union after President Lincoln was elected?

   A) North Carolina
   B) South Carolina
   C) Georgia
   D) Alabama
   E) Mississippi

The correct answer is B:) South Carolina.

99) Which of the following did the Emancipation Proclamation NOT do?

   A) Freed slaves behind Confederate soldier lines
   B) Allowed free African American's to join the army
   C) Allowed free African American's to join the navy
   D) Freed slaves in border states
   E) None of the above

The correct answer is D:) Freed slaves in border states.

100) The quote "Rather than love, than money, than fame, give me truth," by Henry David Thoreau is characteristic of

   A) Transcendentalism
   B) Utopianism
   C) Deism
   D) Abolitionism
   E) Both A and D

The correct answer is A:) Transcendentalism. The American Transcendentalist movement placed emphasis on life, and transcending from animal or worldly impulses, to more spiritual impulses. Henry Thoreau and Ralph Waldo Emerson are the most famous members of the movement.

101) One of the premiere scientists of his time, _____ began studying electricity in 1746.

   A) Thomas Edison
   B) Matthew Stewart
   C) Linnaeus
   D) Benjamin Franklin
   E) None of the above

The correct answer is D:) Benjamin Franklin. One of Benjamin Franklin's most well-known ideas was his proposal to prove lightning was electricity by flying a kite into a storm.

102) An advocate for both the liberation of all slaves as well as women's rights, _____ began publishing The Liberator in 1831.

   A) Frederick Douglass
   B) Sarah Gaines
   C) Andrew Jackson
   D) William Lloyd Garrison
   E) None of the above

The correct answer is D:) William Lloyd Garrison. William Lloyd Garrison and Isaac Knapp co-published The Liberator from 1831-1900. Their circulation was approximately 3,000, 75% of which were African Americans.

103) After the War of 1812, President _____ turned his attention to the Barbary Coast Pirates, resulting in the Second Barbary War.

   A) Thomas Jefferson
   B) James Madison
   C) James Monroe
   D) John Quincy Adams
   E) None of the above

The correct answer is B:) James Madison. In 1815, the United States went to war with Tripoli, Tunis, and Ottoman Algeria. At the end of the war, the U.S. and England stopped paying tribute to the Barbary Coast states.

104) Located in the _____, Mound People built large earthen mounds for religious, ceremonial, burial, and residential purposes.

   A) Southeast
   B) Northeast
   C) Southwest
   D) Northwest
   E) None of the above

The correct answer is A:) Southeast. "Mound People" refers to a collection of cultures in the southeast United States. Mounds built by these cultures have been found throughout Mississippi and Louisiana.

105) Originally published in two volumes, Little Women by _____ details the lives of the four March sisters during the Civil War.

   A) Louisa May Alcott
   B) Mary Elizabeth Braddon
   C) Harriet Beecher Stowe
   D) Rosa Nouchette Carey
   E) None of the above

The correct answer is A:) Louisa May Alcott. Little Women was loosely based on Louisa May Alcott's life with her three sisters. It was published in two volumes in 1868 and 1869, then as a single volume in 1880.

106) Prior to completing and publishing his dictionary, Noah Webster worked as a _____.

   A) Philosopher
   B) Doctor
   C) Teacher
   D) Composer
   E) None of the above

The correct answer is C:) Teacher. Noah Webster taught in Glastonbury, CT after graduating from Yale in 1778. He left the position due to harsh working conditions and low pay.

107) Charles Sumner used the phase "rape of a virgin territory" in a speech regarding the addition of _____ to the Union.

   A) Oklahoma
   B) Kansas
   C) Nebraska
   D) Arkansas
   E) None of the above

The correct answer is B:) Kansas. A state senator of Massachusetts, Charles Sumner argued passionately for the admission of Kansas as a free state. He denounced the "Slave Power," the political arm of slave owners, as wanting to spread slavery into free states that had made it illegal.

108) What two political parties made up the Second Party System?

- A) Democrats and Republicans
- B) Democrats and Whigs
- C) Democrats and Labor
- D) Democrats and Know-Nothings
- E) None of the Above

The correct answer is B:) Democrats and Whigs. The Second Party System refers to a period in the 1800s where the two primary political parties were the Democrats, led by Andrew Jackson, and the Whigs, comprised of National Republicans and other opponents of Andrew Jackson.

109) Phyllis Wheatley was the first published African-American female _____ in the U.S.

- A) Novelist
- B) Poet
- C) Theologian
- D) Journalist
- E) None of the above

The correct answer is B:) Poet. Phyllis Wheatley was born in West Africa and sold into slavery at seven or eight years old. She learned to read and write while with the Wheatley family, and became the first published African-American female poet in 1770.

110) One commonality between slaves and indentured servants was the ability to _____.

- A) Request lighter duties
- B) Get an education
- C) Keep their families together
- D) Work off their passage
- E) None of the above

The correct answer is D:) Work off their passage. Both indentured servants and slaves could earn their freedom by working off the cost of their passage.

111) In 1675, drought and the _____ inspired the Pueblo uprising against the Spanish governor.

A) Assassination of the Pueblo chief
B) Arrest of forty-three medicine men
C) Attack by the Apache
D) War with the Comanche
E) None of the above

The correct answer is B:) Arrest of forty-three medicine men. The Spanish government ordered the arrest of forty-three Pueblo medicine men for sorcery. Four men were sentenced to death by hanging, with three sentences carried out (the fourth committed suicide). The remaining men were imprisoned and publicly whipped.

112) A leader of the Great Awakening, _____ was an itinerant minister who preached at a series of revivals.

A) George Whitefield
B) Benjamin Franklin
C) Jonathan Edwards
D) John Wesley
E) None of the above

The correct answer is A:) George Whitefield. George Whitefield was a founder of Methodism and the Evangelical Movement. The 1740 revival meetings at which he preached became known as the Great Awakening.

113) _____ was the leader of the United Society of the Believers in Christ's Second Appearing, also known as the Shakers.

A) Mother Teresa
B) Mother Superior
C) Mother Ann Lee
D) Lucy Wright
E) None of the Above

The correct answer is C:) Mother Ann Lee. Mother Ann Lee emigrated from England to the U.S. in 1774 with a small group of followers. The group was called "Shakers" because they shook with ecstatic dancing during worship services.

Test-Taking Strategies

Here are some test-taking strategies that are specific to this test and to other CLEP tests in general:
- Keep your eyes on the time. Pay attention to how much time you have left.
- Read the entire question and read all the answers. Many questions are not as hard to answer as they may seem. Sometimes, a difficult sounding question really only is asking you how to read an accompanying chart. Chart and graph questions are on most CLEP tests and should be an easy free point.
- If you don't know the answer immediately, the new computer-based testing lets you mark questions and come back to them later if you have time.
- Read the wording carefully. Some words can give you hints to the right answer. There are no exceptions to an answer when there are words in the question such as always, all or none. If one of the answer choices includes most or some of the right answers, but not all, then that is not the correct answer. Here is an example:

    The primary colors include all of the following:

    A) Red, Yellow, Blue, Green
    B) Red, Green, Yellow
    C) Red, Orange, Yellow
    D) Red, Yellow, Blue
    E) None of the above

    Although item A includes all the right answers, it also includes an incorrect answer, making it incorrect. If you didn't read it carefully, were in a hurry, or didn't know the material well, you might fall for this.
- Make a guess on a question that you do not know the answer to. There is no penalty for an incorrect answer. Eliminate the answer choices that you know are incorrect. For example, this will let your guess be a 1 in 3 chance instead.

What Your Score Means

Based on your score, you may, or may not, qualify for credit at your specific institution. At University of Phoenix, a score of 50 is passing for full credit. At Utah Valley University, the score is unpublished, the school will accept credit on a case-by-case basis. Another school, Brigham Young University (BYU) does not accept CLEP credit. To find out what score you need for credit, you need to get that information from your school's website or academic advisor.

You can score between 20 and 80 on any CLEP test. Some exams include percentile ranks. Each correct answer is worth one point. You lose no points for unanswered or incorrect questions.

 Test Preparation

How much you need to study depends on your knowledge of a subject area. If you are interested in literature, took it in school, or enjoy reading then your studying and preparation for the literature or humanities test will not need to be as intensive as it would be for someone who is new to literature.

This book is much different than the regular CLEP study guides. This book actually teaches you the information that you need to know to pass the test. If you are particularly interested in an area, or feel like you want more information, do a quick search online. There is a lot you'll need to memorize. Almost everything in this book will be on the test. It is important to understand all major theories and concepts listed in the table of contents. It is also very important to know any bolded words.

Don't worry if you do not understand or know a lot about the area. If you study hard, you can complete and pass the test.

To prepare for the test, make a series of goals. Allot a certain amount of time to review the information you have already studied and to learn additional material. Take notes as you study-it will help you learn the material.

Legal Note

All rights reserved. This Study Guide, Book and Flashcards are protected under US Copyright Law. No part of this book or study guide or flashcards may be reproduced, distributed or stored in a retrieval system, or transmitted in any form or by any means, electronic, mechanical, photocopying, recording, or otherwise, without the prior written permission of the publisher Breely Crush Publishing, LLC. This manual is not supported by or affiliated with the College Board, creators of the CLEP test. CLEP is a registered trademark of the College Entrance Examination Board, which does not endorse this book.

FLASHCARDS

This section contains flashcards for you to use to further your understanding of the material and test yourself on important concepts, names or dates. Read the term or question then flip the page over to check the answer on the back. Keep in mind that this information may not be covered in the text of the study guide. Take your time to study the flashcards, you will need to know and understand these concepts to pass the test.

Virginia Dare	**Ponce de Leon**
1492	**London Company**
Separatists	**Mayflower**
Mayflower Compact Agreement	**Puritans**

Spanish explorer that "discovered" Florida	The first English child to be born in the New World
Right to settle Cape Fear, North Carolina and north to Long Island	Columbus landed in the New World
Ship with 101 pilgrims for America	Dissenters from the Church of England
Dissenters who wanted to purify the Church of England	Pledge to obey their own created laws

Massachusetts Bay Company	**Roger Williams**
Thomas Hooker	**Henry Hudson's task**
New Amsterdam is now known as	**William Penn**
Quaker	**Another name for Philadelphia**

Founded Rhode Island	Puritan Colony
Find a shorter route to East India	Clergyman - settled Hartford, CT
Settled Delaware	New York City
City of Brotherly Love	Religious Society of Friends

George Calvert	**James Oglethorpe**
Treaty of Paris	**Intolerable Acts**
Stamp Act	**Thomas Jefferson**
George Washington	**James Monroe**

Settled Savannah with debtors	Secured Maryland's charter
Coercive Acts - Punitive laws put on the colonies by England	Brought the war to a halt in the New World
A chief architect of American Democracy	Required all legal documents, pamphlets, playing cards, contracts, newspapers, etc., to carry a tax stamp
Era of Good Feeling	1st President of the United States

At the birth of the nation, most people held what occupation?	Who first attempted to unite the colonies?
Whig Party President	2 Party System Today
Colonist	Immigrants
E Pluribus Unum	Washington Irving

Benjamin Franklin	Farmers
Democrat and Republican	Martin Van Buren
People who settled in America after the American Revolution	People who settled in America before the American Revolution
Rip Van Winkle and The Legend of Sleep Hollow	Out of Many, One

13th Amendment	**14th Amendment**
15th Amendment	**Abolitionists**
Albany Plan of Union	**Alien and Sedition Acts**
Anne Hutchinson	**Anti-Federalists**

Ensured due process and equal protection under the law, defined citizenship and declared that the US government would not pay compensation for freed slaves.	Officially ended slavery in the United States.
People who were critical of slavery and were in favor of abolishing it.	Guaranteed citizens the right to vote.
Heavily criticized Acts passed under John Adams which outlawed publishing criticisms of the government and gave the president the power to deport non-citizens.	A plan proposed by Benjamin Franklin which would unify the colonies, though they would remain under British rule.
A group opposed to the Constitution because they feared it gave too much power to the Federal Government. Also instrumental in the creation of the Bill of Rights.	Founder of Portsmouth, Rhode Island after religious persecution forced her to leave.

Articles of Confederation

Bacon's Rebellion

Bill of Rights

Boston Massacre

Boston Tea Party

Christopher Columbus

Continental Association

Crispus Attucks

Angry that the governor was not protecting them, a group of colonists led by Nathaniel Bacon forced the governor to leave and began attacking Indian groups.	The United States' first constitution, focused on avoiding problems associated with a strong central government.
In 1770 a group of angry colonists started throwing rocks and snowballs at British soldiers. The soldiers fired their muskets and a few colonists died.	First 10 Amendments to the Constitution.
Spanish explorer who discovered North America in 1492 while search for a sea route to the Far East.	In protest of the new tax on tea, a group of colonists threw an entire shipment of tea overboard to stop colonists from buying the tea and paying the tax.
The first to die in the Boston Massacre. Considered the first martyr of the Revolutionary War.	Created by the First Continental Congress to pressure Britain into repealing the Coercive Acts. Allowed enforced non-importation of British goods.

Democracy in America	**Dred Scott Case**
Eli Whitney	**Eliza Lucas Pickney**
Emancipation Proclamation	**Emma Willard**
Era of Good Feelings	**Federalists**

Dred Scott was a slave who sued his owner when he moved to a free state. The Supreme Court ruled that he had no right to sue because he was property.

A study on the political and social structure of the United States written by Alexis de Tocqueville.

The person who first introduced indigo and made it a successful cash crop in the South.

Creator of the cotton gin which reinforced the importance of slavery for Southern states.

She worked her whole life for the education of women and both instructed teachers and taught female students.

A document issued by President Lincoln during the Civil War which freed slaves in all areas of rebellion.

The political group which supported the passage of the Constitution.

A name for President Monroe's two terms. A period characterized by strong nationalism, economic growth, territorial expansion and a lack of partisan conflicts.

First Continental Congress

First Great Awakening

Francisco Pizarro

Half Way Covenant

Headright system

Hernando Cortez

House of Burgesses

Hudson River School

A religious revival in the mid 1700s which focused on a personal and emotional approach to religion.	A group of delegates which met in 1774 to discuss a solution to oppressive British rule and the possible uniting of the colonies.
A document set up in early Puritan colonial communities which allowed the children of partial church members to be baptized.	Spanish conquistador who conquered the Incan civilization in the 16th century.
Spanish conquistador who conquered the Aztec civilization in the 16th century.	Allowed 50-100 acres of land to be awarded to anyone who brought an indentured servant to the colonies.
Both the first functioning art school in the United States and the name given to an art movement which focused on landscapes.	The governing body set up in Virginia. It was the first legislative body in the Americas.

Democratic-Republican Party was renamed	**Jamestown**
John James Audubon	**John Rolfe**
Kansas-Nebraska Act	**King Phillip's War**
Louisiana Purchase	**Manifest Destiny**

The first successful English colony which was organized by the London Company in 1607.	Democratic Party
The person who is credited with first successfully cultivating and exporting tobacco.	A self-taught painter famous for his collection of paintings of birds.
Created the territories of Kansas and Nebraska and allowed the respective residents to determine their own slavery status.	A series of battles fought in New Hampshire between the colonists and Indians after colonists began settling on Indian lands.
Colonists believed that America was destined to grow west. This was considered a divine right and stewardship.	A land purchase from the French which doubled the size of the country in 1803.

McGuffey Reader	**Mercantile System**
Missouri Compromise	**Monroe Doctrine**
Natural Rights Theory	**Peter Zenger**
Phillis Wheatly	**Powhatan Confederacy**

The economic system of colonial times which judged economic prosperity by the supply of gold and silver. The government strictly controlled trade.

The standard reading textbook for schools in the mid-nineteenth century.

Forbid European countries from further colonization in the Americas.

Admitted Missouri as a slave state and Maine as a free state. Created a line dividing the country into slave and free areas.

He was a newspaper editor that was sued for printing libelous information, but won on the defense that if it was true it wasn't libel.

A theory of John Locke's which stated that all men were entitled to certain natural rights - life, liberty and property.

A collection of Native American tribes which was especially prominent in the Virginia area in the 17th century.

The first African American woman to make a living from her writing.

Pueblo Revolt of 1680	**Roanoke**
Walt Whitman	**Salem witch trials**
Saratoga	**Second Continental Congress**
Second Great Awakening	**Sojourner Truth**

Early English settlement organized by Sir Walter Raleigh which was discovered mysteriously abandoned. 	The Pueblo Indians' fight for independence from the Spanish. 
When teenage girls began to accuse middle aged women of witchcraft. 	Wrote Leaves of Grass 
Drafted and signed the Declaration of Independence. 	The turning point of the Revolutionary War which convinced the French to aid the colonist's cause. 
A traveling preacher who advocated the rights of women and slaves who gave the famous speech "Ain't I a Woman?" 	A religious revival in the early 1800s which focused on a personal piety and not doctrinal knowledge. 

Son's of Liberty	**Lincoln was assassinated by?**
Transcendentalists	**Treaty of Guadalupe Hidalgo**
Triangular trade	**Uncle Tom's Cabin**
War of 1812	**William Penn**

John Wilkes Booth	A radical group formed in 1675 which opposed British rule.
The treaty which officially ended the Mexican American War.	A movement which placed emphasis on life, and transcending from animal or worldly impulses to more spiritual impulses.
Harriet Beecher Stowe	A set of shipping lines that connected Europe, Africa and America in colonial times.
The person responsible for founding Pennsylvania.	When Britain began capturing American ships and forcing them into the navy the War of 1812 began.

www.ingramcontent.com/pod-product-compliance
Lightning Source LLC
Chambersburg PA
CBHW081833300426
44116CB00014B/2569